My imperfect "PERFECT LIFE"

THERE'S POWER IN THOSE HANDS

BY JENNY DYER

First Published 2025 by Jenny Dyer
For further information
contact through facebook page
WALKING WITH WILDLIFE.

Text and lyrics: © Jennifer Dyer 2025
Artwork © Jennifer Dyer

All rights reserved. No part of this publication may be reproduced, stored in a retrieval system, or transmitted in any form or by any means electronic or mechanical, or by photocopying or otherwise without prior written permission of the author or copyright holder.

ISBN 978-1-7640280-1-1

Cover and Artwork: Jenny Dyer (unless otherwise stated.)

> Here I am dreaming again. I can see my story as a musical with an old, old lady with dementia lying in bed asking her daughter the story of her life and her playing all her songs to her so she could remember her musical life and being able to openly feel what her life felt like. The songs were being performed under spotlight around the stage … maybe even putting some commentary in from the old lady to her beautiful daughter and granddaughter.
>
> If this does happen and you do have to put me in an old-age home will you make sure I have a copy of my book and all my songs available on YouTube or a memory stick for the nurses to play to me. Hopefully this will make my old age a bit more fun.

No I'm not doing this for the money. Just enough for my expenses would be good so I can keep writing. I'm not doing it for the notoriety either because no-one would want to be famous for this. I'm writing it to try and stop it happening again to some little girl out there. It's too late for me but may not be for other children.

This is about a true love story punctuated with sadness and I guess there's more to come in the future as that's what life's about.

It's not a book that you can sit down and read in one sitting from cover to cover. If you do a search on YouTube with my name and the song name you should be able to find the music. Please take the time to immerse yourself in the music. My lyrics are so much easier to listen to and read when sung encapsulated in music.

Just this morning I asked my husband if he liked a song he was playing. It was one of his favourites but when I asked him why he liked it he told me he liked the rhythm and the beat. So then I asked him what it was about and he told me war. Not a favourite time for anyone. People have been writing about love and tragedy since year dot.

To my family: Do you want this censored even more to show a beautiful rosy life like I'd been doing for many years or leave it as it is and leave in the parts that really made me the person I am today.

My imperfect "PERFECT LIFE"

By the way…. oh I forgot what I was going to write. Am I getting dementia? Will I follow my dreams?

TABLE OF CONTENTS

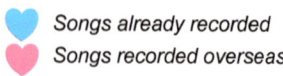
💙 Songs already recorded
💗 Songs recorded overseas

Pink Roses	10
Can't Look In Those Eyes Can You? 💙	13
A Soul That Needs Cleansing (Passion In Me) 💙	14
Music … It Taught Me A Lot (Feelings) 💙	16
How Could You Love The Unlovable 💙	18
Beautiful Eyes 💙	20
After the Exhibiton	22
Dark Eyes (Duet)	22
Psychedelic Blue 💙	24
Wise Man 💙	26
Crying Silent Tears	29
Who's Afraid Of The Big Blue Wolf	30
Bucking Hell 💙	40
In The Old Mango Tree 💙	44
Cherish Every Day 💙	46
True Blue	48
Walk A Mile In A Man's Shoes 💙	49
My Guardian Angel	50
Sweet Little Angel 💙	52
Message From My Heart	55
Proud Independent Man 💙	56
Just Say Sorry (I Trusted You)	60
I Take People As I Find Them	62
Hell And Back	64
Daddy's Old Shirt	65
Follow Those Dreams 💙	66
DO NOT CHANGE THIS!!!!	67
Why Don't You Listen To My Feelings?	70
Broken Wings 💙	72
I Need You (I Wake At Night With Tears In My Eyes) 💙	74

So Call Me 75
You're Beautiful 78
Kokoda (Version 1) 82
Make Love To Me 84
Love Letters 86
I've Struck Gold   (Man's Version) 88
Candles And Roses 90
Who's Gonna Free Me 92
Green-Eyed Monster 93
Nature's Symphony 94
He's Got Grit 97
The Devil Ain't Gunna Get My Soul 98
When That Man Sings 100
My Bucket List 102
Wish I Could Feel Your Hugs 103
Lonely Lonely Man 104
Will I Turn Blue 105
Little Children (It's The Free Things) 107
Been on That Sinking Ship 108
You Believe In Me (Perfect Harmony) 112
Russian Roulette 115
Pretty In Pink 116
WHAT'S A FRIEND ANYWAY!!! 118
God I Love That Smile 123
Got A Woman (Man) 124
That Old Piano Heard My Tears 127
Sweet Soul King Of The Blues 129
Left Bleeding And Hurt (Who Can A Kid Turn To?) 131
I Feel Good 133
BURN BROTHER BURN 135
Thank You Lord For Giving Me This 140
I'd Like To Believe 142

Sweet Little Boy .... 💙 144

Amazing Little Grace .... 💙 145

She Loved Me Like No Other .... 💙 146

Come Closer .... 💙 147

One Woman One Man.. 💙 149

That Girl In The Mirror (Forgiveness is the Key) 154

The majority of the songs in this book have been recorded . The ones with a blue heart have been recorded by me with the help of Lee Turner and Claire Adamik and the ones with a pink heart have been recorded overseas by Soundcloud friends. The one with no hearts have been recorded using Mureka.   They can be heard by searching on YouTube for

Jenny Dyer Song Name
For Example
Jenny Dyer Perfect Harmony

Or the playlist of all songs
https://youtube.com/playlist?list=PLEfpcChMv8GqDbo6Nt_37HJWWluUWBto1&si=uw0x1z6d4yDIAZQp

Or you can follow me on  **Facebook Page**
Jenny Dyer Lyricist and find the link
to the full playlist to listen
to videos of the songs.
Jenny Dyer Lyricist

My First Art Exhibition

Wow! My first art exhibition was booked in. My art group were doing a joint display at the local gallery and I was to be one on the contributors, so we each had to choose our own theme. My husband wanted me to paint something nice like roses. I just did these two paintings and he thought it would be a nice theme.

The sizing wasn't correct for the art exhibition, so I had to do five new paintings within the theme.

In March 2015, I had to dig deep for these paintings so I started my series of paintings called BLEEDING ROSES for the art exhibition. (You'll see later why I called it "BLEEDING ROSES".)

I had to look up the meanings behind the different colours of roses to help me decide what to paint ... you will find other symbolism in the paintings too... so look closely. I have a loving but hurt soul and am gradually peeling off the layers of that hurt. Come with me on that journey. Oh wait; I'll give you the meanings of different coloured roses.

White ... purity, innocence
Dark Pink ... appreciation, gratitude, thank you.
Pink ... appreciation
Orange ... enthusiasm
Red ... love

I had to write a little story about myself to be put with my paintings. So I wrote this to be pinned on the wall beside them.

The Art Exhibition

I believe healing can happen through art and music. I've been writing songs for five years. I started painting in January 2014 for the first time and started using painting and songwriting together to verbalise and visualise feelings. For those who want to delve deeper into what is behind my paintings they can read the songs and believe me, I've written more than one song about some paintings.

I share my feelings when you see my art, read my lyrics and hear my songs .... Often exposing my deepest feelings to you. I hope by sharing these with you, that helps you air your feelings too.

I am a self-taught artist using acrylics and I learnt by experimenting to get the desired effect for the feeling I'm trying to communicate ... and of course looking up techniques on YouTube.

Pink Roses

I feel like I'm dancing
Dancing in a field of flowers
I'm sending out pink roses
Can you feel their power.

Sending out pink roses
Pink roses for the beauty
Sending out pink roses
Pink roses for my friends
And I'll save a perfect rose
For a love so true
And I will save one pink rose
just for you

A rose for perfect harmony
One rose for you to sing
A pink rose for you and me
I got a rose for everything

I raise up my hands
Up to the bright blue sky
I got this feeling
I'm feeling so high

Can you feel its power
The power in the pink rose dove
Can you feel that power
The power in my love

Sending out pink roses
Pink roses for the beauty
Sending out pink roses
Pink roses for my friends
And I'll save a perfect rose
For a love so true
And I will save one pink rose
just for you, just for you

Copyright Jenny Dyer April 27, 2015

The painting on the next page was called STOLEN ... a white rose was a symbol of innocence.

Stolen

Can't Look In Those Eyes Can You?

CHORUS
I can't look in those eyes, can you
Could you sit across the room from a wolf so blue
Could you hold your anger in
Would you call me a coward not to confront him

If she looks into those eyes she'll remember when
She was cracked and broken
If she looks into those eyes she'll remember when
She wants to say the words unspoken
She wants to say the words

If she looks into those eyes she'd tell you
All the hurt and pain he caused
If she looks into those eyes she'd tell you
Because of him, she'd always felt flawed
Because of him, she'd always felt flawed

BRIDGE 1 *She's afraid of those feelings she has*
Sometimes she gets angry as
So she avoids looking at you
What do you think she should do
What do you think she should do

CHORUS

Those eyes they follow you everywhere
Do they make you feel uneasy
Do we live in a world that doesn't care
Hope not cause that wouldn't please me
Hope not cause that wouldn't please me

BRIDGE 2 *How many white roses are picked and taken*
More than you think if I'm not mistaken
Can you look at those eyes and say you don't care
Do you prefer to remain blissfully unaware.

CHORUS
Would you call me a coward not to confront him

Copyright Jenny Dyer May 7, 2015

A Soul That Needs Cleansing (Passion In Me)

You tell me I got a soul that needs a cleaning
You tell me I should confront my demons
You tell me you think you know what you see
But behind that blue is no fairy story

You know it ain't no bed of roses
We have to deal with what life throws us
Bit by bit I'm peeling off my layers
A few rusty feelings are gunna be stayers

I got this passion in me
Opens up my heart
for all to see
Tells my story in colour and song
Tells my story right or wrong
Just where do I belong

I might have a soul that needs cleansing
Don't need to face my demons to be mending
People out there doing it on their own
Afraid to talk in their own home

People out there suffering silently
Thinking they feel differently
Those people need understanding
They don't need society's branding

I got this passion in me
Opens up my heart
for all to see
Tells my story in colour and song
Tells my story right or wrong
Just where do I belong

No I ain't got a black heart
Just a lot of ugly feelings to impart
It's not a vendetta to get him
But yes I'm going out on a limb

Gunna be dragging out the past
Gunna hit like a bomb blast
But if it helps one lost soul
My story is worth being told

I got this passion in me
Opens up my heart
for all to see
Tells my story in colour and song
Tells my story right or wrong
Just where do I belong

Copyright Jenny Dyer May 19, 2015

Music … It Taught Me A Lot (Feelings)

Music … its taught me a lot
Music … sometimes all that I've got
I sit down with my guitar
My best friend by far

She shares my feelings with me
Makes me feel happy
I ain't no Mozart
But that guitar it opens up my heart

As soon as I begin to strum
Those feelings out they will come
Like a river of melting snow
The ice breaks and begins to flow

CHORUS
Feelings Feelings
No longer locked up and choked out
Feelings Feelings
Not too many
Care what they're about

Music … it taught me
Taught me a lot
I don't care whether you love me
So love me or not
Oh yeah I'm gunna sing
Sing about everything
Not gunna tie it up
In a contorted knot

CHORUS
Feelings Feelings
No longer locked up and choked out
Feelings Feelings
Not too many
Care what they're about

BRIDGE
My old guitar
Hears every bar
She just plays along with me
She never disagrees
Sure makes my feelings sound good
Just like a sweet soul mate should.
Yeah Just like a soul mate should.

CHORUS
Feelings Feelings
No longer locked up and choked out
Feelings Feelings
Not too many
Care what they're about
Care what they're about

Copyright Jenny Dyer May 12, 2015

The next rose was Red for Love.

How Could You Love The Unlovable

How could you love the unlovable
But you did
You bought her a rose every day
You stood by her in her darker days UH-HUH

You thought she was lost to you my friend and
You didn't know what to do
You bought her a rose every day
And she threw it back at you

You're a good man
Travelled many a rough road
I know you understand
What it's like to carry that heavy load

So many times she walked beside you
To take a bit of that weight
Enough to get you through
When you had too much on your plate

You thought she was lost to you my friend and
You didn't know what to do
You bought her a rose every day
And she threw it back at you

She couldn't understand
Why you waited so long
It didn't happen as you planned
And she couldn't stay strong

She carried more than you thought
The weight it was too much
Those memories, the final straw
Boy did she need your love, your love, your love, your love

How could you love the unlovable
But you did
You bought her a rose every day
You stood by her in her darker days

You thought she was lost to you my friend and
You didn't know what to do
You bought her a rose every day
Until she said I love you
Until she said I love you
I love you

Copyright Jenny Dyer May 31, 2015

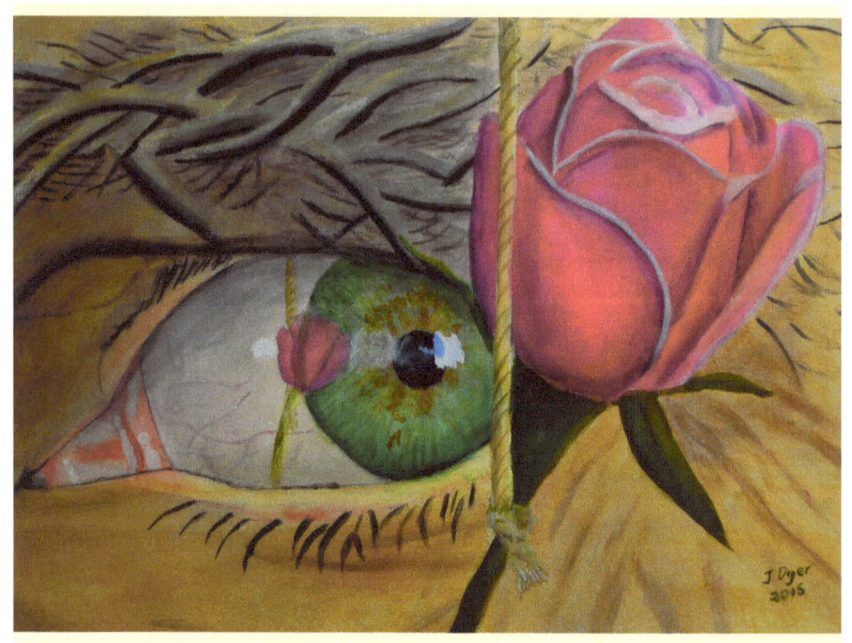

Beautiful Eyes
(Just A Few Scars)

INTRO You know I've never asked you this

When you look into my eyes tell me what do you see
Do you see their colour green or blue
Do you really look at me
And see how much I love you
Look in my eyes tell me what do you feel
Do you feel warm all over
Do you see a soul that's finally healed
Can you feel my love flow over

Beautiful eyes
Just look .. real deep
Beautiful eyes
That's a love you can keep.
Pink roses that's what you are
Perfect happiness with just a few scars.

Can you see love hanging from a thread
Can you see the passion I've got
Can you see how I'm looking ahead
Can you see I'm no longer tied with a knot

BRIDGE:
I can stand alone
I can hold you up
You'll never be alone
You'll always have my love

If you look real carefully
You'll see the hidden gold
If you look real carefully
You'll see eyes never grow old

Beautiful eyes
Just look real deep
Beautiful eyes
That's a love you can keep.
Pink roses that's what you are
Perfect happiness with just a few scars.

So look in my eyes my dear friend
Sometimes my face looks sad
You'll see a love that never ends
You will see the love that I have

Do you feel it looking at you
It's a love that will help you heal
When your days are hard to get through
In those eyes the love you will feel

Beautiful eyes
Just look real deep
Beautiful eyes
That's a love you can keep.
Pink roses that's what you are
Perfect happiness with just a few scars.

Copyright Jenny Dyer June 7, 2015

After the Exhibiton

Dark Eyes (Duet)

Those secrets hidden in my mind
They're seeping through the cracks
Bad memories bit by bit
They're coming back

Once hidden even from me
What unlocked the latch
New vision now I see
Like someone struck a match

**Oh dark eyes, what are you thinking?
Why do you look so sad
Your life, it's been a breeze
Look at everything you have**

I'm thinking…   What would you know
Never walked my path with me
Don't judge cause you haven't seen
Everything that's happened to me

It might look like I've had an easy life

But what would you know
Those memories that were hidden
Well now they're wanting to show

Oh dark eyes, what are you thinking?
Why do you look so sad
Your life, it's been a breeze
Look at everything you have

My dark secret it's hidden inside
Just how do I let it out
He has no idea how I cry
So I just blurt I out

Oh dark eyes I had no idea
You carried that all alone
I woulda been there
Dried up your tears
If only I had known
If only I had known

BRIDGE
You know I can't tell the worst of it
Not even to you
I only have hints of memory
Can't work out if they're true

Oh dark eyes I had no idea
You carried that all alone
I would have been there
Dried up your tears
If only I had known
If only I had known

Can you see the power in my hands
One day I'll work it out
No blood, no tears but I'll understand
I'll know what it was all about

Copyright Jenny Dyer June 15, 2015

This next song was written for True Blue, a special friend who helped me through. I remembered the nickname!

Psychedelic Blue

Looked at that painting on the wall
Reminds me of when I had a fall
You reached out to me brother
And gave me a hand
You told me gently
People would understand

**Because you ….. you pulled me through
From the land of psychedelic blue
You say come what may
You say follow me to a more colourful day
Wow ow ow … see the love in the air
Wow ow ow … pretty colours everywhere
Floating on a bed of blue, yellow and green
No darkness to be seen**

Oh you know my favourite colour is red

I'll always remember what you said
Don't know how it could
But that painting makes me feel so damn good
Just sitting looking at you
Hanging on my wall of blue
There's love in that helping hand
Shows me that you understand.

**Because you ….. you pulled me through
From the land of psychedelic blue
You say come what may
You say follow me to a more colourful day
Wow ow ow See the love in the air
Wow oo ooo Pretty colours everywhere
Floating on a bed of blue, yellow and green
No darkness to be seen
Because You ….. you pulled me through
From the land of psychedelic blue
You say come what may
You say follow me to a more colourful day
You say come what may
You say follow me to a more colourful day**

Copyright Jenny Dyer August 20, 2014

Wise Man

Lived my life with just a little sin
Not always proud of where I've been
Glad that journey bought me here to you
You always know just what to do

You wouldn't try to harm a fly
But there's people, I can't deny
Who will always try to bring you down
But you keep your feet firmly on the ground

**Wise man,
you live by Buddha's rule
Don't try to convert the fool
Wise man,
you know your mind
Oh yeah you're one of a kind**

Those thoughts were going through my head
So I looked up what Buddha said:
Life is full of suffering
Just live with what today will bring

Don't you stress about the past
Or what the future will cast
Just enjoy your life's fruits
Search for knowledge and the sacred truth

**Wise man,
you live by Buddha's rule
Don't try to convert the fool
Wise man,
you know your mind
Oh yeah you're one of a kind**

So Wise man, yeah wise man
So Wise man, yeah wise man
Tell me is that what you do
To stop yourself feeling blue

Wise man,
you live by Buddha's rule
Don't try to convert the fool
Wise man,
you know your mind
Oh yeah you're one of a kind
You're one of a kind

Copyright Jenny Dyer July 2014

Crying Silent Tears

CHORUS

**You got me crying silent tears
Crying silent tears
I use my words but they're never heard
I'm crying silent tears
I'd like to say but can't find the way
I'm crying silent tears
Oh crying silent tears**

You try to push me
You try to convince me
You take away my gems
You try to mould me
Try to control me
But I am what I am

CHORUS

If only I could be heard
If only I could be heard
Do I have to paint a picture
Instead of using my words

CHORUS

One day the dam will break
And the flood will wash me away
When will you ever learn
To listen …
I mean really listen
To what I've got to say
Well I'm gunna do it my way
I'm gunna do it my way
I'm gunna do it my way

Copyright Jenny Dyer April 19, 2015

Who's Afraid Of The Big Blue Wolf

That was her castle
She was dreaming as kids do
She could fight off a thousand men
Hell yeah, that's what she'd do

It was a place she took her friends
Wooden swords for the fight
That's where they'd pretend
To win battles with the black knights

Who's afraid of that big blue wolf
Is he coming to get you
Don't turn your back on him kids
Cause that's what he will do

Tracks around imaginary cliffs
Where only the brave would go
Fight off monsters from the myths
Who died in the valley below

Every kid has their castle
Hers made of hessian and string
She built her world with no hassle
Imagining everything

Who's afraid of that big blue wolf
Is he coming to get you
Don't turn your back on him kids
Cause that's what he will do

So why does that place make her sad
Cause that's where she lost her rose
The most precious thing she had
Why she lost it .. heaven knows

That's where her white knight
Turned into a wolf so blue
He stole the magic of childhood
Cause she didn't know what to do

Who's afraid of that big blue wolf
Is he coming to get you
Don't turn your back on your kids
Cause that's what he will do

White rose for someone special
But it was taken away
Blue wolf from hell
Made it her saddest day
Made it her saddest day

Copyright Jenny Dyer June 12, 2015

(I will take my grand children for a walk by there one day and tell them about our imaginary life. I'll show them the rugged cliffs, how to make a cubby house out off hessian and string and how we learnt to swim in the cattle trough! Yep, in a big round cattle trough. Maybe I should take them over to the gully while it's got water in it and show them how we caught yabbies. How to make a wooden sword? I'd better do it soon.)

TRIGGER WARNING!!
THE BACK-STORY

It wasn't until I was in my fifties and I saw two lovely innocent little eight year old girls playing so innocently together that I realised IT WAS NOT MY SHAME! It was his. How can little kids the age of these two sweet girls know that someone they trust would betray that trust and sexually abuse them. That was the day I had my first of many panic attacks. Who is protecting the children?

He left the area when I was about ten. No more abuse or so I thought. He came back a few years later for a visit and tried to put his hands on me explaining that he had to teach me so my boyfriends wouldn't leave me. He said I needed to know how to keep them happy. He went to touch me again and show me what was ideal and I screamed at him to keep his hands off me or I'd tell my mother. I never did tell her what he had done. I wish she had known why I always called him the big bad wolf. She said "I" was mean when I said that.

When we had gatherings all would be great until HE turned up on the scene with his dirty, inappropriate, crude jokes which made me cringe. But no one knew his dirty little secret because I knew what it would do if they found out, (not even my husband).

It affected my marriage as well. I can remember when my daughter was young I couldn't even completely trust my own husband to stay in my daughter's room to put her to sleep even though I knew he was a good man. I would sneak in and check on them. This shit carried on throughout my whole life.

My daughter would want to go on sleepovers but instead I would invite the girls all to my place in an attempt to protect her. I don't think she's ever forgiven me for not allowing her to go to one particular sleepover at a place where I didn't trust the mother because of her promiscuous behaviour and my daughter was still in primary school and there were older boys going to be at this sleepover. I hope when she finally reads this book she understands.

My husband, who was friends with the person who abused me, would often go away for work. My husband would tell me if I had any problems to get him to help me. He didn't know what pressure he was putting on me telling me to ask HIM for help. No way did I want anything to do with this leech.

We'd often go to visit him for a cuppa. I would have to listen to his inappropriate jokes. He also used to moralise and get on his high horse about what should be done to young criminals who broke the law. Of course, he had all the answers, until one day I said "What would you do to people who sexually abuse children". I saw the look on his face and the guilt in his eyes. I often wondered if he thought his dirty little secret wasn't as safe as he thought it was.

So often I would have to leave fun times because he was there saying his inappropriate comments. I couldn't stand it but I was ashamed that I let this creep touch me. An eight year old child!!! Shamed my entire life. How could I tell anyone what HE DID! Bloody sleaze bag. (excuse my french) How could I be civil to HIM! Yes I threw insults at him and he knew why but it was me still getting in trouble from my mother for being cruel to our visitor. Little did she know what he did to me all those years ago … yes she thought it was me being mean. I so wanted to tell her before she died but it would have broken her heart so I wore the criticism but still couldn't change my attitude towards him. I was seen as the bad person for not treating him nicer. It was all so unfair but they didn't understand because I never spoke up for myself.

"Be brave" I'd say to myself … but here I am still not telling anyone. Now, I am letting the cat out of the bag. This predator of society, oops Freudian slip, pillar of society will be wondering whether I will say anything!

I would sit and write songs to express my feelings about my journey through the shame of child abuse to feelings of low self-worth. Words I couldn't say without music and rhyme. I would sing them over and over again as a form of self-healing. I taught myself to do art to express how I felt then I'd sit and look at those paintings and write songs about them. Sometimes I'd just write the songs about what I was feeling or worried about. Some good, some not so good.

Have you ever had to tell someone something so disgusting about yourself? I needed help to work through it. I had to tell my husband why I was so sour while were driving to visit him. My husband was talking about the tragedies in his family (and he had a few). He made a comment that I wouldn't understand what it was like. I blurted out at him "At least you weren't sexually-abused, were you?" and asked him to take me home. I couldn't go there one more time.

Do you know how hard it is to say those words, those disgusting words, out loud to your husband? A dirty secret I'd never told anyone... a disgusting secret I felt I could never share because people would think horrible things about me. Why did it bubble up so many years later? I still have no answer for that but I was starting to think about it all the time. It made me feel SO DISGUSTING.

I went looking for a photo to try and determine how old I was at the time. You know I can even remember my mum giving me the lecture when I was a kid. I asked my mum if I was beautiful and she told me I'd never be beautiful. I may be pretty but I'd NEVER BE BEAUTIFUL. When I saw the photo that's when I wrote the song YOU'RE BEAUTIFUL to that little girl. So I'd spent my whole life thinking I wasn't beautiful.

He made me think she was right: I'd never be beautiful. He told me no one would like me if I didn't know about sex. He had to teach me. Yuk, he stole MY INNOCENCE. I will never forgive him for that. It changed my whole life. People kept telling me you should forgive but I CAN NEVER FORGIVE WHAT HE DID TO ME. It's still too disgusting to write the details down in words. My confidant at the time was my music teacher as I think a lot of broken people turn to music when they are badly hurt. He read it in my lyrics. Somehow it helps you express those feelings. I don't think my family understands why I spent so much time and money recording my songs. My teacher was the one who told me I should tell my husband and that if I was his wife he'd want to know.

I need a break. Writing this book was starting to get a little heavy so I grabbed my camera and decided to go walking with wildlife. I'll be back.

While I was away I took some amazing photos. .. Yes, I have to pace myself so I don't get too upset.

The photos I took, while I was on my walk, was a reminder to me that even nature can be cruel but even the snakes in life can get eaten.

NOW BACK TO MY STORY My walks were my way to relax. Now even that was disturbing for me at the time as sometimes he drove past me when I walked. I would dread him stopping to say hello. He didn't know I'd told my husband and brothers and anyone else I thought needed to know. I didn't want to talk to him. I still don't want to ever talk to him again. One day he is going to die. I don't even want to go to his funeral but what will people think of me not turning up to his funeral. What will his wife and kids think? To this day, they still don't know. I will have to go for them.

Even as I'm writing this book I don't know if I can share it with the world but my daughter deserves to know why I was an over-protective mother. Sorry but I couldn't bear the thought of anything like that happening to her.

When I see hurt people I often wonder what secret they have that messes with their head.

While I'm writing this story I'm praying that it's not going to send me down a dark path again like it did all those years ago. I wonder how many hurt people out there in the world walk this same precarious path and will they end up in the same mess I did years ago while I was trying to process and communicate, even with myself, to try and get over the very personal hurt I felt.

Just WHY WOULD PEOPLE ALLOW THIS in our society. Why does society allow children to be left in that dangerous situation? Imagine the damage it would cause to someone if it was a family member who hurt them and they were the reason they were taken away from their family. Either way damage is done!!!!   And what if no one believed them. OMG how tragic!

(Just had a funny thought. Maybe psychologists will read these messed-up thoughts of this once-abused child to study the effect of abuse on children. Heck, even now I have trouble admitting I was "sexually" abused as a very young child.)

My mother always told me I was lucky in life. It used to bug me because I didn't feel lucky! She had no idea.

I'd blocked out a lot of memories from my childhood. Is that how our mind works when we've been abused to help us cope with the trauma? Slowly as I revisited my youth those horrible memories were coming back. Song lyrics, put to music sound so much better than those bitter words like I just shared with you. Music and singing helps. My songs weren't meant to be little La-de-da country songs either.

So this back story has been written at night too. I get pain and I write until the pain goes away. A bit like I did years ago when I wrote all the lyrics. But then I had a different type of pain. I'm slowly piecing my story together but it's taken a bit of research and talking to my supportive brother. I've had lots of different medications to get rid of the pain but the side effects of them isn't good. Some actually caused Parkinson's type reaction. I had the shakes. If I didn't get off that medication none of my children's story books would have been written as I wouldn't have been able to use my camera with the shakes like I had as a side-effect of the drugs.

My first ever song

The first song I wrote was to promote a coffee table book called Rodeo Downunder. On the way home in the car one night, I'd think of a line, so I'd stop and write it down so I wouldn't forget and by the time I did my usual 15 minute journey home from town I'd actually written a song that made the Hot Country charts, my first song!

As I was proofreading this I realise this was actually the second song I wrote. I can remember singing a silly little song I wrote (four lines long - not bad for a little kid ... and it rhymes too) as I rode my bike to school and I bet my brother still remembers the words of it ... he heard it so many times it drove him crazy. LOL.

Now back to my first recorded song.

Bucking Hell

Flags are flying, our cowboy's prayer
Champions line up, the arena out there
Clear the ring, here comes the action
Watch the bull, fatal attraction.

Put on your boots, strap on your chaps
Stretch your legs, for the cowboy tap
Spit on your hand, get yourself psyched
It's a better bull, than you woulda liked

**Bucking hell and hooves that thunder
Ready to Rodeo Downunder
Bucking hell bucking thunder oh
Yeah Rodeo Downunder**

Up in the chutes, slipping down
Wrap that rope, round and round
Oh come on boy let's slide to ride
This bull's a little on the wild side

Open the chute, we're ready to rock,
Dig in the spurs, for the cowboy rock
Lay back cowboy in a trance
Ready to do the bucking bull dance.

**Bucking hell and hooves that thunder
Ready to Rodeo Downunder
Bucking hell bucking thunder oh
Yeah Rodeo Downunder**

Crowd are cheering, buckin up high
Spurring from front to back side
Go for it boy hang in there
Lost your grip thrown through the air

Pick yourself up bulls don't play fair
Rodeo boy don't stay down there
Pick yourself up, Cowboy down
Troubles brewing, send in the clown

**Bucking hell and hooves that thunder
Ready to Rodeo Downunder
Bucking hell bucking thunder oh
Yeah Rodeo Downunder**

Chick in tight jeans, cowboy at her side
looking for more than an 8 second ride
Each rodeo champ is out for money
Likes to have his own buckle bunny

**Bucking hell bucking thunder oh
Come on babe let's Rodeo Downunder
Bucking hell bucking thunder oh
Come on babe let's Rodeo Downunder**

Copyright Jenny Dyer May 28, 2008

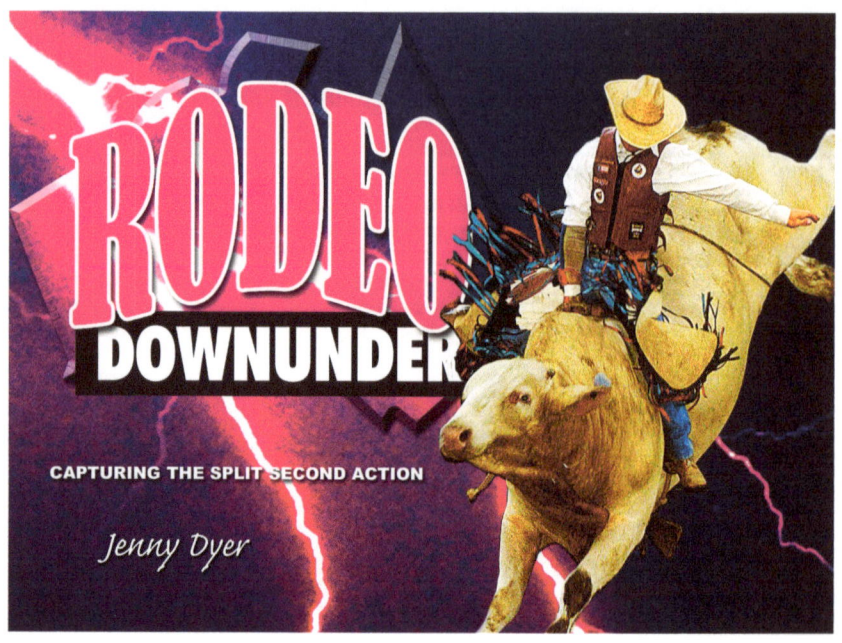

I actually gave my lyrics to three local singers I knew.

One decided he knew better and changed my lyrics but that wasn't on, how dare he change my story, it wasn't his to change, so I tossed his version. A singer has no right to change my story.

After asking advice from a music teacher I taught with years before, he sent a young lady along to me and she sang the lyrics exactly as I wanted. She did an amazing job on this rock song and her version was played at many rodeos I went to.

The second version was done by a local country singer. Because I had trouble deciding which version to use, I played both versions of the songs and the consensus of my friends was that the country version was the best so I promoted it all over Australia and the song actually made it to the hot country music charts. He went on to record his own songs and added my song to that album.

This musical journey was one of discovery for me. I learnt so much about myself and it brought back so many memories, good and bad, as I wrote.

When we were kids we had a cubby built in the old mango tree near my home. When I was young I used to sit up there and look out over Dad's wheat fields … well, the song will tell you the rest.

Yes I changed the lyrics of Mango Tree from man to woman so my music teacher didn't feel like he was gay singing it. Then I started wondering why I used to hide in the old mango tree.

In The Old Mango Tree

Sitting on top of the old mango tree
Sitting in a place where I'm safe as can be
Watching the wheat wave in the breeze
The best view that I could seize.

I feel so safe sitting up here
No one could conquer that fear
The old mango tree was solid and sound
I was sitting twenty foot from the ground

I'm up here in the old mango tree
Hiding where no one else could see
Dreaming of things that I would do
Dreaming about me and you.
About me and you

I'd hide up there where I couldn't be seen
I'd sit up there and continue to dream
I dream about the life that I would lead
I dream about the things that I would need.

I dream about the things that I would do
I dream about the people like you
I dream about the years to come
I dream about the things to be done

I'm up here in the old mango tree
Hiding where no one else could see
Dreaming of things that I would do
Dreaming about me and you.
About me and you

The tree house is no longer there
The mango tree no longer bears
But I've found myself a new solid tree
In the arms of the wo/man I dreamed I'd see

A wo/man with a solid heart of gold
A wo/man I'd live with till I'd grow old
The wo/man with the arms that surround me
Like the branches of the old mango tree.

I'm up here in the old mango tree
Hiding where no one else could see
Dreaming of things that I would do
Dreaming about me and you.
about me and you
Dreaming of things that I would do
Dreaming about me and you.
About me and you
About me and you
About me and you

Copyright Jenny Dyer July 2009

Such a sad time

Then my husband's sister was troubled. Her husband left her and she became unstable and my husband and his brother would travel 400 km to take turns to stay with her for support. I was working full time and looking after the property while he was away. This was so tiring. It was my dad's birthday so she was left alone for one day only in which she took her own life.

My husband took it so very hard. I was so worried about him. He was so depressed ... couldn't answer the whys, what if's, so many unanswered questions. She was very religious and we couldn't understand how she could go against her beliefs. That's what inspired me to write my second recorded song. My husband loved it. 'Nice one, Jen!'

The singer sang it beautifully but after he finished it, his partner told me not to give him any more of those deep feeling, soppy songs. Why, I don't know but it was obvious I was going to have to sing my own songs in the future.

Cherish Every Day

She left us there that very night
She couldn't see there would be light
We wish we could make her see
Good life comes from misery
(Misery)

Cherish every day you've had
Tell your friends when you are sad
Tell your family that you care
Tell your friends you're always there
Always there

We miss her so very much
Her brilliant smile, her friendly touch
I would do just anything
To bring her back to hear me sing.
 (hear me sing)

Cherish every day you've had
Tell your friends when you are sad
Tell your family that you care
Tell your friends you're always there
Always there

Don't try to do it on your own
It's much easier when you're not alone.
We love you, we need you
We need you to go beyond blue.
(beyond blue)

Cherish every day you live
You have so very much to give
 Cherish every day you live
You have so very much to give
Much to give..

Oh let us help let us care
Let us help to get you there.
 (Oh let us help let us care
Let us help to get you there.)
 (let us care)
let us care
Let us care

Copyright Jenny Dyer 2010

When she passed away, I blamed my brother-in-law (who was a cheat). I thought he was the reason she took her own life. Such a sad time. I don't think there is any death that is as hard to take as suicide. So many unanswered questions.

True Blue

I'm very grateful to have a friend like you
You have a special gift - you are true blue
You had faith when others doubted
It makes me so happy I want to shout it

A friend is someone who understands you
A friend is someone who's always true blue
A friend is someone who helps you grow
A friend like you everyone should know

I love the sounds you help me create
I love the way you help me communicate
You listen to all the things I said
You help me create the music from my head

A friend is someone who understands you
A friend is someone who's always true blue
A friend is someone who helps you grow
A friend like you everyone should know

Everyone should have a friend like you
Someone who cares and is true blue
You understand music is good for the soul
You understand that it comes from the feelings we hold.

A friend is someone who understands you
A friend is someone who's always true blue
A friend is someone who helps you grow
A friend like you everyone should know

Copyright Jenny Dyer September 2009

Do you also know I wouldn't be here today without True Blue's help. Thank you my friend.

Walk A Mile In A Man's Shoes

Walk a mile in a man's shoes
Before you try to criticize
The type of life that he would choose
And the reason for his lies

We all make our own decisions
Along the bumpy road yeah yeah
We carve our path with precision
We all have a heavy load
We have a heavy load

Walk a mile in a man's shoes
Before you try to criticize
The type of life that he would choose
And the reason for his lies

We all take our own track
To the pearly gates ah hah
Where we can't look on back or
Be judge of our mates.
Or be judge of our mates.

Walk a mile in a man's shoes
Before you try to criticize
The type of life that he would choose
And the reason for his lies

We all make our own mistakes
Accept us for what we are, good Lord
We don't get no double take my friend
to pass the judgment bar
pass the judgment bar.

Walk a mile in a man's shoes
Before you try to criticize
The type of life that he would choose
And the reason for his lies
I said the reason for his lies
The reason for his lies

Copyright Jenny Dyer May 2010

My Guardian Angel

My guardian angel knew my road would be bumpy
But he was still there to guide and help me
He put the ideas in my head
For what needed to be said

He played the music to the songs I could hear
To help me face the parts of life I fear
He helped me share those things I'd been hiding
He guided me to the soul mate to confide in.

I hope one day I can find the words I need
To thank the guardian angel who helped me be freed
I hope one day I can find the words to say
I want to thank him every single day

He's a master craftsman with such skill
He knew my journey was all uphill
He knew I needed help along the way
He knew just the right thing he had to say

My guardian angel was a true musician
He teaches his craft not by tradition
He teaches his craft with such feeling
He knows that music deals with whole body healing

He knows that songs are the key to inner peace
He knows that music can give such release

I hope one day I can find the words I need
To thank the guardian angel who helped me be freed
I hope one day I can find the words to say
I want to thank him every single day

Written 5 am this morning after a good nights sleep - thank God - Copyright Jenny Dyer May 6, 2010

Losing a precious child

So the first and only song I sang and recorded was "Sweet Little Angel". My husband's sister's little boy was diagnosed with brain cancer before he turned one. We spent so much time driving down to support her with her heart-breaking journey. They had four other children to look after as well and the darling little angel had to travel to 1000 kilometres regularly for cancer treatment. What a really sad time that was? I can remember one day when I was down in Brisbane with Cathy that her precious baby started choking and she panicked and laid him on his back on the bed screaming at him to breathe. I took over and just rolled him into recovery position and it cleared his throat and he started breathing again.

About six months later, when he passed away I got a lady to paint his portrait as an angel and I sat down and wrote this song. So off I went to my music teacher knowing absolutely nothing about singing, never been trained and asked him if he could help me record this song. It took me six months of recording to even get it close to acceptable and not very close at that. Of course I wanted a rock song because I was angry that such a sweet little angel would be taken at such a young age. So after the six months I gave the song to Cathy and she never liked it because it wasn't a sweet little song like her little boy. She liked my words but not the singing.

So I failed! No more singing for me. I had spoilt a good song. I was going to record it again for her but I never did. I just moved forward.

I didn't paint this painting on the next page but it was copied from a photo I took of her little angel so she could remember how sweet he was. The artist even made his sick little face look bright and cheerful. I did some research on Facebook and was able to track the artist down for permission to use it in my memoir. After this my daughter reacted by becoming an oncology nurse. What an amazing person she has become! Oh just so you know, she was always amazing.

Painted by Glenda John

Sweet Little Angel

You were little not very old
No one should hear the news she was told
Nothing could break a mother's heart
Like hearing the news she'd have to part

Sweet little angel

She watched your little life fade
We watched her life turn to shade.
You were here for such a short time
Making you leave was such a crime.

Remake

Sweet little angel

**Angel in heaven above
Time was short so much love
Sweet little angel
Angel in heaven above
You live on in your mother's love
Sweet little angel
Sweet little angel**

Sweet little angel

We hope she'll find joy
With memories of her boy
Memories of the love that she gave
Memories we need to save

Sweet little angel

You live in your mother's love
A love given from above.
A love which only grows
A love which a mother knows

Sweet little angel

**Angel in heaven above
Time was short so much love
Sweet little angel
Angel in heaven above
You'll live on in your mother's love
Sweet little angel
Angel in heaven above
Thank you for your sweet love.
Sweet little angel
Sweet little angel
I've been touched by an angel
Touched by an angel**

Copyright Jenny Dyer February 22, 2016

My sister-in-law recently showed me this little song I can hardly remember I wrote.

Message From My Heart

You keep knocking I'm not home
My mind tends to go on roam
You think I'm sitting in this space
But I'm really in some other place

Thinking about what I've done wrong
Sitting here writing this song
Thinking about what is right
My mind and heart are having a fight

Well here's a message from the heart
I can't bear to be apart
You're the one I know it's true
I wanna live my life with you

I get sad but there's no need
You wouldn't make my heart bleed
When you're near I know its true
And for this I thank you

I'd like to make you understand
My mind sometimes gets out of hand
But you really need to know
You're the one that makes me glow

Well here's a message from the heart
I can't bear to be apart
You're the one I know it's true
I wanna live my life with you

You're the one
I know it's true
I just wanna
Be with you

Copyright Jenny Dyer March 16,,2009

My Men on the Land

I wrote the next song and sent it to a young up-and-coming country musician. I thought she had talent and I was right. She has since gone on to become a country music star winning song writing competitions. **But she changed my lyrics and the song was no longer my story,** so I canned the idea. It was my story and she shouldn't have changed it without my permission. After that, I asked my music teacher if he would sing my songs. I was so grateful that he said "yes".

Proud Independent Man

His land was his home his love and his joy
He'd lived there right from when he was a boy
He's a practical man of the earth and
He knows damn well what his life is worth

Just give him a chance give him a hand
Please don't break this man of the land
Like all workers of the land
He won't ask with his cap in hand

**He's a proud independent man
He won't cry "Lend me a hand"
He's a proud independent man
He just wants to care for his land**

We've made things hard for the carers of the soil
We made many problems, we made them toil
We've bought in pests to infest their land
We've bought in weeds they dig out by hand

He's endured the floods and the drought
He can tell you what hardship's about
He's doing the best that he can
To endure an attack from fellow man

He's a proud independent man
He won't cry "Lend me a hand"
He's a proud independent man
He just wants to care for his land

He re-builds the fences, he replants the crops
He carts the feed to his starving stock
He's not a stirrer not a union man
He's a (practical) straight shooting working man

He works hard into the night
No double time was in his sight
He doesn't ask for any wet pay
Just wants a future, he wants his say

He's a proud independent man
He won't cry "Lend me a hand"
He's a proud independent man
He just wants to care for his land

When they're all gone - They're a dying breed
Who's going to be there to plant the seed
It's not the drought it's not the flood
That takes the farming out of our blood

Bring back our future
Bring back our right
Bring back our future
Give us some light

Bring back our future
Bring back our right
Bring back our future
Give us some light

Copyright Jenny Dyer April 2009

So our musical partnership began. I wrote this song that day and afterwards I painted an old, black and white photo of my father ploughing with horses and put colour into it. My little brother liked the painting so I gave it to

him. To this day it hangs on the wall of my little brother's home, even though he has passed away.

The song was written primarily about my father but also about the other farmers in my life. I can't remember exactly why I wrote it but it was to do with some stupid government legislation that affected farmers very badly. I had four farmers very close to me, my dad, my little brother, my brother-in-law and of course, my husband, all very independent men who just wanted to work their land. So I put pen to paper and decided to tell the politicians what-for! So "Proud Independent Man" was born. The first song of our song-writing partnership. I wrote the lyrics and he created the music and sang them. I will be forever grateful for that.

By the way, the government still aren't looking after the man on the land. One day they may not have the food to feed the people.

Then out of the blue, I wrote this song to HIM, the man who hurt me so badly, wanting him to say sorry to me for what he had done to me. I gave him this song to read. Yes he did say sorry. Too little too late, he was an old man and should have said sorry by himself a long time before without being asked.

Just Say Sorry (I Trusted You)

What you did was a crime
You'll live with that till the end of time
There's nothing you can say to me
Except to say you're sorry

It's just one word but it means that
You would want to take it back
And take away all this pain
So I can be happy again

I trusted you you hurt me
I want you to say sorry

You're secret's safe I won't tell
It's just my little piece of hell
I can forgive but not forget
You haven't said sorry yet

It's just one word and it's a start
A sorry said from the heart
Without that sorry I can't heal
Without that sorry I can't feel

I trusted you, you hurt me
I want you to say sorry

You've got family I've got mine
And their future we define
I'm trying hard to adjust
To a life without trust

Its always in - in my mind
One like you they may find
Some one who they can't trust
Some one who is not just

I trusted you you hurt me
I want you to say sorry

You took my youth, you took my pride
You made me feel bad inside

You did me wrong, you should regret
You haven't told me sorry yet

It's just one word but it means that
You would want to take it back
Take away all this pain
So I can be me again

(loudly You've been hurt)
I trusted you, you hurt me
I want you to be sorry

I trusted you you hurt me
I want you to say sorry

(Softly)
I trusted you you hurt me
I want you to say sorry

Copyright Jenny Dyer April 26, 2009

I later changed the chorus to:

You know what
It's no longer how I feel
I don't need your damn sorry
To trust and heal
You know what
It's no longer what I said
I don't need your damn sorry
To get you out of my head

I Take People As I Find Them

I take people as I find them,
I call a spade a spade.
I take people as I find them,
I know when I'm being played.

I don't care what they look like
As long as they treat me well,
I don't care what they look like
or if they never do well.

I take you as a friend
and friendship is a must.
A friend is someone special
... someone you can trust.

I take you as a friend
and you'll know I'll care
I'll take you as a friend
So please treat me fair

I take them as I find them,
They've all got a story to tell.
I take them as I find them,
They've all had their own piece of hell.

I take the time to listen.
I take the time to hear.
I take the time to listen.
To listen without fear.

I take you as a friend
and friendship is a must
a friend is someone special
... someone you can trust

I take you as a friend,
and you'll know I'll care,
I'll take you as a friend,
So please treat me fair.

I don't judge them by their looks
or the colour of their hair.
I don't judge them by their shoes
or the clothes that they wear.

I don't judge them by their house
or the type of car they drive.
I'd like to know they're happy
and glad to be alive.

**I take you as a friend
and friendship is a must.
A friend is someone special
... someone you can trust**

**I take you as a friend
and you'll know I'll care
I'll take you as a friend
So please treat me fair**

Special friends are like diamonds
so very rare.
Much more precious
than any jewel out there.

Copyright Jenny Dyer May 2009

Hell And Back

I've been to hell and back
It's one long hard track
It's been so much pain
Don't want to go again.

I've been such a fool
I shouldn't loose my cool
You think I'd bite my tongue
And just look for fun.

**Yeah I've been to hell and back
That's one hard track
Hell and back
Hell and back**

I think I've lost my touch
I shouldn't say so much
Tuck it safe away
And think before I say

I should box it in
Some tidy little bin
Bolt down the lid
And keep my feelings hid

**Yeah I've been to hell and back
That's one hard track
Hell and back
Hell and back**

Copyright Jenny Dyer July 2009

I wrote this song after my dad died. I was so sad to have to watch him go. It was days in the palliative care ward. He was an upstanding man. He always fought for what was right. His advice still stays with me. "You'll live and learn."

Daddy's Old Shirt

I wore Daddy's old shirt since he was gone
The elbow's worn through and now it has gone
I wanted something to keep him close and near
I just wanted to have him stay here.

They said I'm Daddy's Little Girl
All wrapped up in my own little world
Yeah Daddy's little girl
With her own little world

It was blue and grey and made of flannel
But bought back memories of the strength that he'd channel
The strength he'd share with our mother and us
The strength he showed all without fuss

CHORUS

We bought him the coat cause he felt the cold
He said it was cause he was getting old
We can't all stay forever young or
there'd be many a song that'd never be sung

CHORUS

Copyright Jenny Dyer July 2009

I was starting to question whether I should be writing my songs, so I wrote this song. This is the advice I gave to myself.

Follow Those Dreams

Is there a door, I didn't open
Is there talent? I keep hoping.
Hope I found out what I'm meant to do

I'm searching for a reason
There are chances to be seizing
To live a life that's meant for you

**You gotta follow those dreams
and they'll follow you
You gotta follow those dreams in the
hope that they'll come true**

So many things out there you see
Will I find the one meant for me
With my life, I'm being true?
I know that I'll feel rich
When I find my perfect pitch
And then will all my dreams come true

**You gotta follow those dreams
and they'll follow you.
You gotta follow those dreams in the
hope that they'll come true**

I would like it to be said
I liked the life I have lead
I did the things I dreamt that I would do
I'm searching for a reason
There are chances to be seizing
To live a life that's meant for you

**You gotta follow those dreams
and they'll follow you
You gotta follow those dreams in the
 hope that they'll come true**

You gotta follow those dreams
and they'll follow you.
You gotta follow those dreams in the
hope that they'll come true
You gotta follow those dreams in the
hope that they'll come true

Copyright Jenny Dyer August 2009 Altered July 2012

Just so you can see how this old mind works I wrote this at three in the morning.

This is how it comes out of my head ... NO EDITING!!

DO NOT CHANGE THIS!!!!

My dream was to put my lyrics to music and I accomplished that pretty well with my music teacher and also with my overseas friends who I never met. Katja was one of them. It was so much easier talking to someone you didn't know. I had many conversations with Katja.

My dream now is to tell my story to the world just in case it could help one little girl. Oops I nearly thought about writing lyrics again.

I want to tell my story to the world just to save at least one little girl. I'm going to write another book ..: oh wait I remember that now. I've already written it years ago. I wonder if there's enough words there. I can't do every thing at once. I'm going to write another bucket list.... Later. One step at a time for me.

But this book is going to be in two versions an e-book which will be free and printable so every kid has access to it or printed book in case someone wants one (this one won't be free.) I'm going to need a psychologist advice when I'm writing this one. Yep and I do know one. I wonder if she'll help me. Thoughts to ponder on. Oh and yes she's a singer but I don't like to ask her because she is so busy. I wonder who else. I could do it. Maybe the books could be given out free to schools as well. Is that a topic for school or at home?

I wish I had someone to help me with my dream. My life can't be for nothing.   I'm an impossible dreamer aren't I.

Mmmm and maybe it could be sung too because kids remember lyrics and song, the best. I'll have to think about that one too. I lay that question in the lap of the Gods.

Aren't I lucky to look at my lyrics again. Will I ever be able to achieve this before I die, have I left it too late. Will my problem-solving skills get me there. Would my family understand why I need to do this? We'll see! I may have to change or rewrite parts of the book to make this possible.   Yep, my mind does work in strange ways. I'm not the same as everyone else. (You're getting the thoughts straight from my head). I promise I won't edit this section. Yep, how would you like to live with my absent mindedness.   I'm always getting criticized for it. I can't help it. When I get set on something I like to achieve it. I've done that my whole life. Remember when I started the shop. Oh wait I'm off track again. My minds always working. Time to get some sleep… my pains gone! By the way I don't think my mind stops when I'm asleep as I usually have the solution to my problem when I wake up. Now don't go back and change this. I better write that at the beginning too so I don't change this.

OMG I nearly forgot to send that. I woke up and I was so grateful I had lost my message. Yep I'm typing this on my phone because I'm too lazy to get out of bed to get pen and paper. Now back to sleep. Oh and sometimes I forget the put in the N'T in words like hadn't.

Why Don't You Listen To My Feelings?

Why don't you listen to my feelings
They're not clear to you
Got too many of your own
To try and sort thru
I don't expect solutions
Just want you to see
I just want you to know
What's happening with me

I wish I didn't feel anger
I wish I didn't feel helpless
I wish I didn't feel cheated
I wish I didn't feel sadness
They're caused by things
We can't control
I've just got to let go of
These feelings that I hold

Tell me what you're thinking
I need to know
Tell me what you're feeling
Just let it show.
You'll have to trust me
You know that I care
Haven't got a crystal ball
Haven't seen what's there

Feelings of loss and pain
feelings of jealousy
Caring about someone else
More than me
I try to sort my feelings
It's way too complicated
It's way too difficult
Peace of mind's over-rated

Tell me what you're thinking
I need to know
Tell me what you're feeling
Just let it show
You'll just have to trust me

You know that I care
Haven't got a crystal ball
Haven't seen what's there

I'm feeling very angry
I'm feeling very blue
I'm feeling betrayed
All these feelings true
I just want to feel secure
I want to feel whole
I want to feel happy
I don't want to feel cold

I just want to feel loved
Bad feelings eat your soul
How can I let go
Of these feelings that I hold
It's not that you don't care
Cause I know you do
So why aren't you listening
Aren't they important to you?

Why don't you listen to my feelings
They're not clear to you
Is it because
I'm not telling
... not telling you?

Copyright Jenny Dyer September 2009

No-one wanted to read my lyrics. It was just a silly old lady writing stupid songs. But they were much more to me. Oh no, I lie. My friends on Facebook listened. Well some of them. My friends on Soundcloud listened too. BTW <u>My songs were my feelings</u> just in case you didn't know.

The next song was sung by one of my rodeo friends. I met her when I was photographing at a rodeo. We connected with it at some level and I sent this song to her. She sang it, recorded it and made the video.

Broken Wings

I was just a fragile butterfly
He broke my wings I could not fly
I needed help but could not cry
I needed help and couldn't say why
I wrapped myself in a cocoon
To shield myself from impending doom
For years that shell remained intact
Until the day it began to crack

The outer wall had broken down
I saw a king with a broken crown
Like a butterfly with a broken wing
I flapped around till I learnt to sing
I emerged like a mocking bird
I'd sing about it, every word
But the hardest song I'd ever sing
Was about the man who broke my wings

I want to fly like a butterfly
I want to sing like a mocking bird
I want to fly like a butterfly
I want to sing it every word

I'll sing about the love I felt
I'll sing about the cards I was dealt
I'll sing about my daily life
I'll sing about my personal strife
I'll sing about my favourite man
I'll sing about this beautiful land
I'll sing about friends I had met
I'll sing about my personal threat

But the hardest song I'll ever sing
Is about the man who broke my wings
The hardest song I'll ever sing
Is about the man who thought he was king
He broke my wings when I was young
Before I had any songs to be sung
He is now old and he is grey
Life's not easy for him I'd say

One day he'll meet his biggest fear
The fear I'd lived with all these years
until that time I'll sing my songs
And I'll not fear what he did wrong.

I want to fly like a butterfly
I want to sing like a mocking bird
I want to fly like a butterfly
I want to sing it every word

Copyright Jenny Dyer November 2009

I couldn't even walk near places without horrible memories coming up when I walked past spots where he had his way. I can't even remember how come I would end alone with him. He must have designed that as a way to get at me. Some memories just won't come back to me.

I was so grateful to have the husband I had. I wrote this song for him.

I Need You (I Wake At Night With Tears In My Eyes)

I wake at night with tears in my eyes
For all the years I forgot to cry
I'm making up for lost time feeling
I know myself I feel I'm healing

You touch my skin it feels alive
I know now I will survive
I should have done this years ago
It didn't show, I didn't know

I didn't know what I'd been in
I didn't know the ice was thin
I should have known it would stand the test
Your love for me is one of the best

CHORUS
I need you
like the flowers need the rain
Shower me with your love
over and over, again and again

I'd give so much but never taken
I should have trusted, I was mistaken
A shared sorrow helped me through
I should have trusted, trusted in you

You're my mate, my best friend
You're my lover to the very end
You're my lover of many years
Shared many wins, so many fears

I feel now we are complete
Our love is so very sweet
As sweet as honey from the bee
I know now what is meant to be

CHORUS

Copyright Jenny Dyer December 2009

The next song, I wrote as an interpretation of what my singing teacher would say to me after writing a particularly painful song. Yes; he was perceptive to know how writing these songs would affect me. I can still hear him saying "Call me." One day I did call him because I hadn't slept for days. He told me to tell my husband and I said I did but he wasn't listening. He said MAKE HIM LISTEN … Probably saved my life.

So Call Me

I'm here for you when you need a friend
Know where you've been - know where it ends
Don't bottle it up – just give me a call
Don't bottle it up you'll hit the wall

So call me – that's what friends are for
So call me – any time at all
You're not on your own just give me a call
Pick up the phone any time at all

My special friend, I know you're hurt
He treated you badly – he treated you like dirt
My special friend, He should know
What he did was wrong, no place to go

So call me – that's what friends are for
So call me – any time at all
You're not on your own just give me a call
Pick up the phone any time at all

Don't let it get you - talk it through
It'll play on your mind it'll destroy you
Don't worry - put it to a halt
What he did was never your fault

So call me – that's what friends are for
So call me – any time at all
You're not on your own just give me a call
Pick up the phone any time at all

Copyright Jenny Dyer February 2010

When You Find Love

You know my son
When you've found someone
Your earth, wind and sun
When you find that soul
Take her and grab hold
And tell her she's the one

When you find love wrap your arms around her
When you find love wrap your arms around her
I tell you son
When you have found the one
Wrap your arms around her
Yeah take her in your arms
Enjoy her many charms
Build a life to surround her

You can travel the world
And not find another girl
That loves you any more
Don't forget to tell her
You cherish and love her
Richer or poorer

When you find love wrap your arms around her
When you find love wrap your arms around her
I tell you son
When you have found the one
Wrap your arms around her
Yeah take her in your arms
Enjoy her many charms
Build a life to surround her

Be brave not afraid
True feelings won't fade
They'll just get stronger
As each day goes by
You'll laugh and you'll cry
Don't wait any longer

When you find love wrap your arms around her
When you find love wrap your arms around her

When you find love wrap your arms around her
When you find love wrap your arms around her

Copyright Jenny Dyer April 2012

(Now I can't sleep at night because of pain. Old age stinks, doesn't it!)

I decided to look for a photo of me from when I was little. Cameras weren't a thing back then and there are not many photos to jog my memory but I did find this one. In fact, there's still not many photos of me. I take photos of people because I want to capture a moment to remember.

When I saw that photo I remember what my mother said when I asked her if I was beautiful and she told me I'd never be beautiful. She was wrong! I wanted to tell the little girl in me that SHE WAS BEAUTIFUL.

You know why I like this song the best. Because it makes my crap story sound good and it told me I was beautiful. Just look at this precious little kid. How could anyone mistreat her! That is so sad.

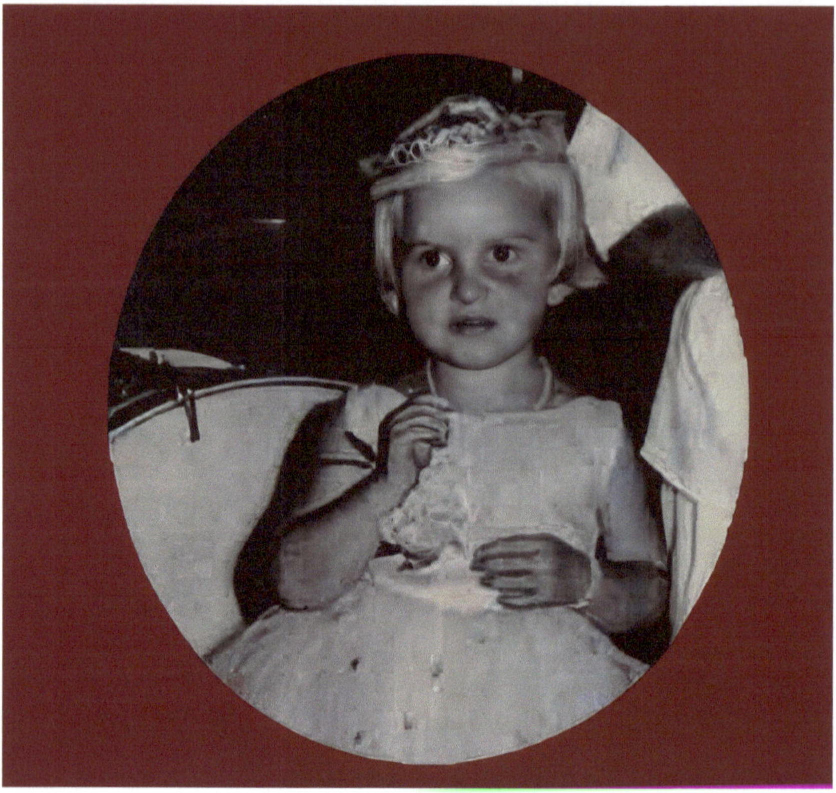

You're Beautiful

Mistreated
Defeated
Stomped on, tromped on
Treated like dirt

I know you've been used
I know you feel so confused
Left with feelings that you shouldn't keep
Left with feelings that will stop your sleep
you're beautiful

You're beautiful oh oh oh so beautiful
You're beautiful oh oh oh so beautiful

As you ask yourself do I belong
Stay safe and keep going strong
As we listen to your many cries

We all want you to realise you're beautiful

You're beautiful oh oh oh   so beautiful
You're beautiful oh oh oh   so beautiful

He did things not taught in school
He broke every golden rule
This message that I'll send to you
Even when you're sad and blue you're beautiful

You're beautiful oh oh oh   beautiful
You're beautiful oh oh oh   beautiful

Beautiful day to be alive
Beautiful day to see the sky
The birds are flying on the wing
Listen to them as they sing you're beautiful

You're beautiful oh oh oh   so beautiful
You're beautiful oh oh oh   so beautiful

A thousand people out on the street
Listen to the rhythm and the beat
No matter what you say and do
There's people that will care for you
you're beautiful

You're beautiful oh oh oh   so beautiful
You're beautiful oh oh oh   so beautiful

Beautiful day to be alive
Beautiful day to see the sky
The birds are flying on the wing
Listen to them as they sing you're beautiful

You're beautiful oh oh oh   so beautiful
You're beautiful oh oh oh   so beautiful
You're beautiful oh oh oh   so beautiful
You're beautiful oh oh oh   so beautiful

Copyright   Jenny Dyer August 2012

Just had the biggest sleep in the endeavour to not go down the path I did last time I tried to write my story when I was working full time but I think I'm strong enough to write it this time and now that I'm retired I can have a day-sleep pretty well any time I need it. Besides my lack of sleep at the moment is caused by a different source of pain.

Every night I end up with stomach or rib pain caused either by a back injury I had when my horse bolted and because of the injury I received when the gynemesh that was inserted in my body to repair a gynaecological problem. (Where would I be without google to check the spelling of these big words). It took a long time before doctors sent me to a specialist to try and determine the source of my pain. I'm sure they thought it was in my head. It only happened because I asked if my problems could have been caused by the gynemesh. There was some publicity about it in the news and I think it was my brother rang me about it after reading about it in the paper. Now there's been a law case that has been going on for ages. The case was won against Johnson and Johnson. It's been many years since all my problems caused by this mesh. The mesh actually wore a hole through one of my internal organs. I had another operation to remove the mesh but it was too late to remove it all as the nerves that go to my legs grew through the mesh.

There's been an initial payout which was pretty minuscule considering the pain I had for many years and the many side problems that it has permanently caused. I await to see if the next payment will allow me to buy another camera.

"Shine Lawyers today welcomed a $300 million in-principle settlement agreement in two class actions

brought against Johnson & Johnson Medical and Ethicon which sought damages on behalf of Australian women who received pelvic mesh implants.

The proposed settlement was reached on 9 September 2022 is the largest settlement in a product liability class action in Australian history, and is subject to approval by the Federal Court.

My husband told me I could spend that money on myself and this is how I choose to spend it. Writing my stories and buying a new camera. A bit frivolous because I don't really need it but I really would like to be able to take action shots (which the camera I use now won't do).

Here it is 2025 and I still haven't received the full payout for injuries caused so many years ago.

I know, but when I die I want to pass that camera on to my grandson and hope he will continue to photograph whatever he thinks is beautiful in his life. He is only nine and got 3rd place against adults for photography in the show. What a future he has if he cares to follow that direction.

My daughter keeps ringing to see if I'm okay. Such a caring and knowledgeable daughter. God, I love her smile.

Back to writing my story now. What a complicated life I've had!

Kokoda (Version 1)

Will he be worrying, will his feet be sore
Will he be struggling under the weight he wore
Will it be enough to break his will
Trudging endlessly up heartbreak hill

Will he survive, will he come back
From that (treacherous) Kokoda track
Where days are hot and nights do freeze
And men catch mosquito borne disease

**He will remember them
each step of the way
He will remember them
And the price that they paid**

Will he sleep dry or will he sleep wet
Smelling and covered in his own body sweat
Will the mud be cold and ankle (knee) deep
Will it cake like lead to the soles of his feet

Will the leeches suck his blood dry
Will the grueling walk make him cry
Will the days of endless drudgery and hurt
Show him how our diggers felt in the dirt

**He will remember them
each step of the way
He will remember them
And the price that they paid**

Will there be food to keep hunger away
Will he suffer each and every day.
Living with only the clothes on his back
Traipsing along that long treacherous track

Will the pain and struggle take its toll
Will it be enough to bare his soul
Will he become another cross on the hill
Because of his persistent and strong will

**He will remember them
each step of the way
He will remember them
The price that they paid**

It's 70 years since the war has been won
Will he remember each and every one
Who gave his life to protect our shore
In that heartbreaking god forsaken war

I feel for those women many years ago
Worrying what's happening, they didn't know
Praying so hard for their man's safe return
It was a lesson, so hard to learn

**We will remember them
each step of the way
We will remember them
And the price that they paid**

Copyright Jenny Dyer July 2012

I wrote this song when my husband and son walked the Kokoda track.

Written for a bit of fun ...

Make Love To Me

What you doing sitting in that chair
Close your eyes and say a prayer
You're gonna need some help tonight
Cause I've got you right in my sight.

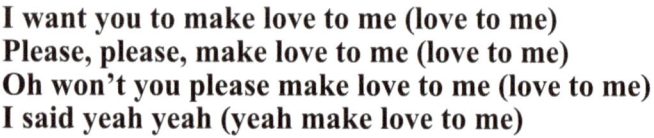

I like the way you curve your lips
I like the way you move your hips
I like the way you hold me tight
Cause I just wanna rock your night (OH yeah)

I want you to make love to me (love to me)
Please, please, make love to me (love to me)
Oh won't you please make love to me (love to me)
I said yeah yeah (yeah make love to me)

I don't wear no angel wings
I don't care 'bout fancy things
I don't need no God dammed money
I just want to please you honey (oh yeah)

I want you to make love to me (love to me)
Please, please, make love to me (love to me)
Oh won't you please make love to me
I said yeah yeah (yeah make love to me)

I like the way you rub my thigh
I like the way you make me try
I like the way you hold me tight
I like the way you rock my night

I want you to make love to me (love to me)
Please, please, make love to me (love to me)
Oh won't you please make love to me
I said yeah yeah (yeah make love to me)

I have to tell you I want your love
I need to tell you I want your ...
I have to tell you I want your love

I need to tell you I want your …
I have to tell you I want your love
I need to tell you I want your …
I have to tell you I want your love
I need to tell you I want your love

Copyright Jenny Dyer July 2012

One day, I was going through my cupboard and I found a whole pile of old letters that I wrote when I was transferred away from my boyfriend (now husband). Another book? He'd kept them all these years.

I started listening to music on the app Soundcloud. There were musicians on there that would do collaborations with others so I started putting my lyrics out into the world. I had so many songs. "Those Love Letters" was one of those songs and was also recorded in England.

Love Letters

I found mine in the office drawer
People don't write letters any more
Tied up neatly with a satin bow
Memories of the love you used to show

Sat out in the morning sun
Read those letters one by one
They took me right back in time
To when our love was in it's prime

CHORUS:

Those love letters
I'd hidden them away
Those love letters
I couldn't throw them away

Oh those ramblings of the heart
Are precious reminders of our start
Two young lovers sharing dreams
On perfumed paper with folded seams

Tender things that you would say
How you were counting down the days
Told me how much you missed me
Can't wait to hold and kiss me

CHORUS:

Those special notes in your own hand
Delivered daily by the postman
They've become treasured memories
Those love letters you sent to me

Signed off with all my love
You're all I can think of
Oh my darling missing you today
Wish you could come home to stay

CHORUS:

Those love letters
you sent to me
Those love letters
are treasured memories

Copyright Jenny Dyer October 2012

I've Struck Gold   (Man's Version)

INTRO
Been digging, looking for gold
To find myself a beautiful soul
Known so many women before
But wanted one that I'd adore

I had women who treated me bad
Women who made me hopping mad
Those type women you want to forget
So I kept looking for my Juliet

Rubba Dub Dub Rubba Dub Dub
I was looking, looking for love
Rubba Dub Dub Rubba Dub Dub
Yeah looking, looking for love
Wanted love that lasts till I grow old
Won't stop looking till I find that gold

Temptation is sent our way
Sent to lead us far astray
I grew up, wanted so much more
So glad you walked through my door

You were a woman with principles
Maybe just a little unpredictable
You treated me good from the start
A pretty woman with a golden heart

Rubba Dub Dub Rubba Dub Dub
I was looking, looking for love
Rubba Dub Dub Rubba Dub Dub
Yeah looking, looking for love
Wanted love that lasts till I grow old
Won't stop looking till I find that gold

Fell on my feet when I met you
Sweet and innocent and so true
I could see that I'd struck gold
So I took you and I grabbed hold.

Women like you didn't come my way

Get to know me, love me any way
Oh yeah, I struck gold
Found myself that beautiful soul

**Rubba Dub Dub Rubba Dub Dub
I found that love, found that love
Rubba Dub Dub Rubba Dub Dub
I found, yeah I found that love
I stopped digging cause I struck gold
Found myself that beautiful soul
Found myself that beautiful soul**

**I struck gold ,,,,, I stuck gold
Found myself that beautiful soul**

Copyright Jenny Dyer December 2012

I've always been creative. When my children were small, sewing was my creativity. I even made a puppet called Basil Brush for my children to talk to when they wouldn't talk to me. When they were hurt, he was a special friend in their life and now the grandkids love him.

The following song I wrote after the Sandy Hook massacre where twenty innocent children and six adults were shot. I sent it to a Soundcloud friend in America. So upsetting to hear that news.

Candles And Roses

The angels cry diamond tears of love
When they take little children up above
Young people with their lives cut short
Gone to live in the lap of the Lord

Broken hearts are always left behind
Praying those angels will be kind
Those little children we no longer hold
Let's light a candle for their soul.

Christmas will come Christmas will pass
But love for that child will always last
The gentle breeze upon your skin
Is their kiss blown on the wind

The angels cry diamond tears of love
When they take little children up above
Young people with their lives cut short
Gone to live in the lap of the Lord

There are so many diamonds in the sky
From when those angels have to cry
They will shine every night
Just to show you they're alright

Those little lives were not in vain
We feel their tears in the rain
They allow new life to grow
So the rivers of love will always flow

Then there'll be rainbows
Beautiful roses will grow
Roses to remind you
Of the love you know

Candles and Roses - Broken hearts
Candles and Roses - Had to part
Candles and Roses - My diamond love
Candles and Roses – Shining in heaven above

The angels cry diamond tears of love
When they took those children up above

Broken hearts are always left behind
Praying those angels will be kind
Those little children we no longer hold
Let's light a candle for their soul

Candles and Roses - Broken hearts
Candles and Roses - Had to part
Candles and Roses - My diamond love
Candles and Roses – Shining in heaven above

Copyright Jenny Dyer December 2012

When I started my business on my own, I used to do all the creative work but as the business grew and grew, I was left to do the proofreading and book work. Both jobs that didn't require any creativity. I was ready to leave but couldn't. I wanted to do something different and creative with my life as I was getting nothing out of it any more.

I wrote the following song when I was trying to sell my business.

Who's Gonna Free Me

This sweet little lady wants to write a song
She's busy, busy, busy all day long
From when the sun begins to shine
Working, working all the time

That work keeps getting in the way
Day after day after day after day
She's got no time, no time, no time
She's needs someone to throw her a line.

CHORUS
She cries "FREE ME"
"Who's gonna free ME? (Free me)
Someones got the key (Free me)
Who can it be (Free me)
Who's gonna free ME?
Who's gonna FREE ME!!
FREE ME (Please, Please, Please)

Time doesn't grow on trees
She can't do as she would please
She feels like a prisoner
She wants life to be simpler

She's got other dreams to follow
Work makes her feel so hollow
She doesn't feel she's doing any good
She's had enough of this neighbourhood

CHORUS

Someone's thrown away the key
So who's gonna FREE ME!!!

Copyright Jenny Dyer January 3, 2013

The next song I sent overseas which was recorded by a Soundcloud friend Katja in Germany.

Green-Eyed Monster

I wish I didn't feel this way
Cause I know you wouldn't hurt me
I have to keep those feelings at bay
But I know what a flirt she can be

I see the way she sidles up to you
Or is it my imagination
Oh and she's my best friend too
But I've really got no justification

CHORUS
The green-eyed monster's coming to get me
Feeding on my insecurity
Cuddle me and make it die
Oh, It makes me wonder why
I let that damn monster in
Jealousy is such a sin!

I tell myself that it's alright
But it eats away at me
It puts doubt in my sight
Is this my insecurity?

I tell myself don't give into it
Your suspicions are unjust
You really have to admit
Its not a relationship without trust.

CHORUS

Your love and cuddles make me secure
Give me more, give me more,
Chase that damn monster away
Cause I don't want it to stay.

CHORUS

Chase that damn monster away
Cause I don't want it to stay

Copyright Jenny Dyer February 10, 2013

I've always liked to walk along my road and I wrote this song about my walk that morning.

Nature's Symphony

Woke up this morning went for a walk
My mind was all wrapped up in thought
I opened my eyes and I looked around
I was treated to nature's surround sound

The crickets giving rhythm with their feet
The bull frogs burping out his beat
The birds flying across nature's stage
Singing free with no cage

CHORUS

Nature's symphony
A performance just for me
Backdrop of mountain ranges
All done in perfect 3D

I look up at that old grey gum
Spot lit from the searing sun
Those fluffy clouds float on by
The painting on the canvas of the sky

Changing art as I walk along
To the sound of the bird's beautiful song
Sometimes I forget to really see
The beauty created just for me

CHORUS

Why do we get so tied up
Walk around with out eyes shut
Our own little world closes in on us
and we can miss oh so much

Got to take a breath and look around
Appreciate my surround sound

The living art that's totally free
Created by nature to hear and see

**Nature's symphony
A performance just for me
Backdrop of mountain ranges
All done in perfect 3D
Backdrop of mountain ranges
All done in perfect 3D**

Copyright Jenny Dyer February 27, 2013

My son who walked across America, then went on to walk across Australia. He always pushed himself. Even though I was very proud of him. It was very worrying. I would love to have this song recorded for him but my singing teacher no longer has his recording equipment and it wasn't recorded at the time. Maybe someone will record it for me by the time I die. Good luck with that one! I would like a song to remember him by when I get old and senile.

NOTES TO MY KIDS: When I'm old, will you show my nurse where my life story is on YouTube so I can remember those I love. I am so sad that I haven't got a song recorded to remind me of the amazing man my son is. Maybe he'll write and record a song for me so I could put it with my other songs. It doesn't have to be flash … just sung by him and recorded on a phone. I would love that for my 70th birthday. Here I am dreaming again but I know he has that talent hidden away. He's a very smart, creative man. Keep on using that creativity in whatever you do.

Walking through the snow with his partner. Brave!

He's Got Grit

Gotta admit, he's got grit
and a lot of determination
He won't balk, he'll try to walk
Right across the nation

He's alone, so he rang home
For a bit of conversation
I could cry, he's parched dry
Suffering dehydration

CHORUS
He's pushing to the limit
To find what his soul's got in it
One step at a time
Till the end of the line
Yeah he's got grit

He's on a path, walking fast
Not looking for a reputation
3000 miles, it'll take a while
To reach his destination

A personal goal, no drum roll
He's not looking for acclamation
But he'll inspire, cause he's a trier
Not lacking in motivation

CHORUS

He crossed the states with his mate
No talk of failure
With his pack, on his back
He's crossing Australia

I'd sing out loud, he makes me proud
He's walking like a machine
This young son, inspires his Mum
The way he follows his dreams.

CHORUS

Copyright Jenny Dyer February 28, 2013

The Devil Ain't Gunna Get My Soul

The devil thinks he's in control
Says he's coming to get my soul
Look out boys ... I'm coming in
Gunna show that devil he can't win

**Get this place out of his control
The devil ain't gunna get my soul
Belt out a tune on your guitar
Get this place out of his control
The devil ain't gunna get my soul
Show the devil how good we really are**

GUITAR BREAK

No use crying cause we're all dying
We ain't never gunna give up trying
I'll win that fight, just hang on tight
The devil won't get me in his sight

**Get this place out of his control
The devil ain't gunna get my soul
Belt out a tune on your guitar
Get this place out of his control
The devil ain't gunna get my soul
Show the devil how good we really are**

GUITAR BREAK

The music won't stop till the devil drops
Let's rock this joint till the roof pops off.
So look out boys ... Here I come
Gunna show that devil just how its done

**Get this place out of his control
The devil ain't gunna get my soul
Belt out a tune on your guitar
Get this place out of his control
The devil ain't gunna get my soul
Show the devil how good we really are**

GUITAR BREAK

The devil won't bet his gold guitar
Cause he knows how good you are
So turn that frown upside down
Its time we ran that devil right out of town

Get this place out of his control
The devil ain't gunna get my soul
Belt out a tune on your guitar
Get this place out of his control
The devil ain't gunna get my soul
Show the devil how good we really are

The devil ain't gunna get my soul
The devil ain't gunna get my soul
The devil ain't gunna get my soul
The devil ain't gunna get my soul

Copyright Jenny Dyer August 2012

I'm not going to tell you where the previous song came from. Some things are just kept secret. Something good out of something bad again.

Once again I turned to Soundcloud to record another song. I wrote the song below while listening to one of the musicians singing and I sent it to his guitarist to help me record it. So awesome these connections I made on Soundcloud at the time.

When That Man Sings

I just listen to the words that he sings
His music makes me think naughty things
I'll just have to wait till my man comes home
Cause this heart has no need to roam

But those guitars play tricks on my mind
Raising emotions that they seem to find
I'll be waiting for my man at the front door
Cause this music has me wanting him more

Oh when that man sings
He makes me think naughty things
Oh when that man sings
He makes me forget my wedding ring

.
I lost my feelings there for a while
I didn't even know how to smile
I had a bad case of the blues
Didn't even put on those walking shoes

I turn up the music in front of me
It is the best blues remedy
It stirs up those feelings in me
That I thought were history

Oh when that man sings
He makes me think naughty things
Oh when that man sings
He makes me forget my wedding ring

He caresses those words with his guitar
Makes you forget where you are
Those sensual sounds slide off his tongue
Makes me believe each and every one

Says he's got something to say to me
Oh I listen so carefully
Says he got things on his mind
His heart break is so defined

Oh when that man sings
He makes me think naughty things
Oh when that man sings
He makes me forget my wedding ring

Copyright Jenny Dyer February 22, 2013

I'd show my music teacher the lyrics and the song I was playing in the background to get the beat and he'd interpret my ideas and come up with brilliant original music. I think that's when my song writing may have improved. I absolutely loved being there through the whole recording process ... coming up with the beat and melody, laying down the tracks (drums, guitar, bass, keyboard and even Didgeridoo once), sitting at his desk while he sang his vocals and then getting my beautiful backup singer in to add her touch at the end. What a great song-writing team!

I love the next song. I love the beat. I love everything about it. I reckon my songs were getting better.

PS I'd encourage you to write your bucket list. It's amazing what you can achieve when you have a direction in life.

My Bucket List

Purple sunset in the sky
That sun looks me in the eye
Smoke haze on the range
My life is about to change
Pushed into a corner
It's just enough to warn ya that ya
You're only here for a speck of time
Do it now not down the line

CHORUS
Gunna write my bucket list
Ten things in life I don't want to miss
Gonna tick 'em off one by one
The last thing on that list
Is to write another one
Write another one

A burning fire inside of me
Cause when I look at my history
I look at what I haven't done
Want to do each and every one
I get my pen and I write it down
Flames flickering around
This excitement it burns me up
Ten things will make the cut

CHORUS

Gunna blow that smoke away
That's no joke, it starts today
I'm breathing in fresh air
Possibilities everywhere!!!

CHORUS
Write another one

Copyright Jenny Dyer February 14, 2013

My daughter left to work in England. When she left I missed her terribly.

Wish I Could Feel Your Hugs

I saw my wishes crystallise
When I had you before my eyes
I prayed for you to come home to me
From that place across the sea

I love feeling your warm hugs
It makes my heart strings tug
No one holds me like you do
But you're gone again and I feel blue

CHORUS
I wish I could feel your hugs
So much love
I'll have to frame your smile
Cause I won't be seeing it for a while

You gave one of those hugs and walked away
Oh how much I wanted you to stay
I know I had to let you go
But I can't help missing you so

You got on that plane, I waved goodbye
I tried so hard not to cry
When will I ever see you again
Oh I don't know when

CHORUS

It makes me so sad and lonely
You live so far away from me
It'd be nice if you could come back
Just can't replace a hug like that!

CHORUS
Want to feel your hugs
Want to feel that love

Copyright Jenny Dyer December 2012

Lonely Lonely Man

The black dogs following in his tracks
But there's no holding him back
He's traveling a long lonely road
And he sure is carrying a heavy load

He struggling with the solitude
But he has a path to which he is glued
No, he won't deviate
Gone too far, it's way too late

But he's a lonely, lonely man
Walking his path on his own
He's a lonely, lonely man
So far away from his home

He's gunna turn failure inside out
He'll push himself without a doubt
How much pain will he endure
He'll not give in, that's for sure

But the black dogs following in his track
Keeps chasing him away but he comes back
When that rain comes teaming down
And he's got a cold bed on the ground

But he's a lonely, lonely man
Walking his path on his own
He's a lonely, lonely man
So far away from his home.

How much hardship
Can one man take
He pushes on
While his body aches

You have to admire
his tenacity
No limit
To this heart's capacity

But he's a lonely, lonely man

Walking his path on his own
He's a lonely, lonely man
So far away from his home.

Copyright Jenny Dyer March 2013

Will I Turn Blue

Will I turn blue if I drink red
Would that wine go to my head
Would it chase away my insecurity
Or would it help my creativity

What would be left unsaid
If I had a little bit of that red
Would I loosen up and bare my soul
Sing about what I can't control.

Would a red fix this old heart
Would it give me a brand new start
Or just give me a damn sore head
And send me early to my bed

CHORUS

Creativity just amazes me
Will that red drop set it free
Should I have a glass or two
To write that song well overdue.

Sob stories written in song
Play on the radio all day long
Will I write one about myself
Or just drink a toast to my health

CHORUS

Twenty-one bottles, twenty-one bottles
Don't you dare let them grow old
In every single bottle
There's a story that's never been told

CHORUS

What would be left unsaid
If I had a little bit of that red
Would I loosen up and bare my soul
Sing about what I can't control.

Would a red fix this old heart
Would it give me a brand new start
Or just give me a damn sore head
And send me early to my bed

CHORUS

Twenty-one bottles, twenty-one bottles
Don't you dare let them grow old
In every single bottle
There's a story that's never been told

In every single bottle
There's a story that's never been told

In every single bottle
There's a story that's never been told

Copyright Jenny Dyer May 2013

Yes, I did drink a few wines back in the day but I haven't bothered with any form of alcohol for years. I don't think it was good for me so I stopped and the most I will do is have a sip of my husband's just to remind myself I didn't need it. His reaction was usually "get your own" but I never did. I'm not using alcohol for a crutch! And yes, some of you drink a bit too much too. This one is for you too!

Artwork Milly Hine

Little Children (It's The Free Things)

It's the free things that make life worth living
It's the free things like the love that you're given
It's the free things like new life for the world
It's the free things like our boy and our girl

Chorus:
Little children, our children
Grown from love's seed
Little children, our children
Love is what they need

It's the free things that bring so much joy
It's the free things not expensive toys.
It's the free things like the smile on their face
It's the free things like that child's embrace

Chorus

They mean so much Oh, their love and their touch
My children I can't do without
These children I love I hold them so far above
Anything else in this world.
Oh how I love my boy and my girl.

Chorus x 2

Little children, our children
Love is what they need

Copyright Jenny Dyer August 2013

Been on That Sinking Ship
What Doesn't Kill You Makes You Stronger

You've got to hold it together
Ride out that stormy weather
If there doesn't seem to be an end
Just be patient my dear friend

No one gets out of the world alive
We're all gonna die
We have to make the best of what we've got
Good things will come out of this bad lot

(What doesn't kill you
Makes you stronger
You just have to wait
A little longer)
Believe me
I should know
Been so far down
You wouldn't want to know

I've been on that sinking ship
I was losing my grip
Just going through the motion
Battling waves in that big ocean

Made myself get out of bed each day
Go about things in the normal way
Prayed for my life to turn around
I got back on solid ground

CHORUS

You've just got to hold it together
Ride out this stormy weather
You've got to hold it together
Things will get better

CHORUS

Copyright Jenny Dyer June, 2013

I was asked to write the previous song for one of the musicians on Soundcloud and this is what I came up with. The heading was to be WHAT DOESN'T KILL YOU MAKES YOU STRONGER.

 well, this is great!!! fantastic lyrics, Jenny!! Loving the music and the vocals are amazing!! Well done to all involved :)

Review number 2

Crackign collab and very well doen by you both here guys. I must admit Deb's appraoch here was entirely different to my original idea and that would of been to get a male singer who has got a cotten picking cowboy voice to put it across. But in the end I felt it still worked pretty well, and very well done my good friend.

I re-recorded it and changed it slightly leaving out a little bit of the chorus and changing the heading to BEEN ON THAT SINKING SHIP.

In this day and age we are connected all over the world. You can achieve a lot if you have the right connections. That's if you're good enough that is.

I put quite a few out into the universe.

I wanted the next song to be a perfect song for my teacher ... perfect pitch cause I knew how particular he was. I loved Adele singing "Rolling in the Deep" and I knew I wouldn't get her to sing my song so I searched Soundcloud to find a singer who could sing it as good as her and I think I found one with Katja Ebert. So I told her my story and she recorded the song for me. So Perfect Harmony was born.

Not what I expected but still lovely. After all, I couldn't get my teacher to sing his own song. I did have to help Katja with the pronunciation though because she is from Germany.

When I showed this song to my husband he loved it because he thought it was for him (and he still loves it). So I re-read the lyrics and yep it could be seen that way but the meaning behind the words would be totally different. Showed me that different people would take different things out of my lyrics.

My teacher once told me the best love songs in the world are ones that can apply to anyone. This one could apply to my friend, my love and also the big man above.

I would love this song sung in all genres of music … is that possible? Just throwing that out into the universe. Me dreaming again! HA HA

One day someone will record it again and that someone was me. On the next page there are links to both versions, one opera and the second one blues.

Perfect harmony - vocals

Jenny Dyer KaT

KaT

You Believe In Me (Perfect Harmony)

You are the music to my songs
You are my beautiful melody
You make me feel like I belong
You bring out the best in me
You believe in me

You are the bow to my violin
You are the strings to my guitar
You make my heart sing
Music flows wherever you are
I love my superstar

CHORUS
I'd like to sing,
sing this song for you
Cause you are a friend that is true blue
I'd like to sing, I'd like to sing
sing this song for you, sing this song for you
A precious friend, that's why I love you

You are a friend who makes me feel rich
Conductor of my orchestra
Puts my life on perfect pitch
Helps me catch those shooting stars
A good friend that's what you are

You are the notes to my masterpiece
Inspired me in my crescendo
Gave me the courage to speak my piece
No worry about innuendo
Without you where would I go.

CHORUS

Perfect harmony
That's what you are to me
Perfect harmony
That's what you are to me

CHORUS

Copyright Jenny Dyer July 2013

The following song, I reckon could be a good one to play at my funeral ...LOL. What do you reckon? "Don't go opening the gates of hell" sung in church. Mmmm. not sure about that. Or maybe it should be "THE DEVIL AIN'T GUNNA GET MY SOUL" Wish me luck on that one.

[JUST A RANDOM THOUGHT OUT OF THE BLUE: You know once I was even planning to go to China to teach but my mum talked me out of it. I'm so glad my children weren't talked out of their overseas adventures even though I missed them terribly and worried about them so much. It's a big bad world out there. "Live your life and do it well, don't go opening the gates of hell" My kids are out there doing that. MAYBE THAT THOUGHT WASN'T SO RANDOM]

Russian Roulette

My wish …. a needle in a haystack
My love … a feeling without payback
My life … a blur without an off switch
My music … a story with a fever pitch

My mind … churning like a whirlpool
Dreaming ….just like an old fool
Wondering … what could have been
If I'd really dared to dream

**CHORUS
Live your life ….. and do it well
Don't go opening the gates of hell.
So many choices you will get
Bit like playing Russian Roulette
Russian Roulettle
Life or death
Choices we take
Make or break**

Always played … on the safe side
Never game …. for the roller coaster ride
Only did … what I thought was right
Always listened to the voice inside

One day at the end of my life
They'll dissect my story with a knife
I hope that they'll be able to tell
I lived my life so dammed well

CHORUS

Oh lived my life so dammed well
So many choices ..
But I didn't open the gates of hell!

Copyright Jenny Dyer 10 0ctober, 2014

Pretty In Pink

CHORUS

She's pretty
Pretty in Pink
Real pretty
Don't you think
As the light shines down on her
I bet you will agree
She's real pretty
Just between you and me Oh
She's pretty in pink
Yeah Real real pretty in pink
Real Pretty in Pink

Funny when we first met
She had a smile you'd never forget
I'd never heard her sing
But fate's a real strange thing

She would cast a spell on you
With the voice of an angel
A friend I'll always keep
We were destined to meet Oh

CHORUS

Beside her walks her man
They walk hand in hand
Yeah he walks tall
 His heart .. brim full

He's loves his lady in pink Oh
He's lucky don't you think
He doesn't need to be told
She's got a million dollar soul

CHORUS

We don't need to be told
She's got a million dollar soul
She's Pretty ,, Pretty in pink

Yeah She's Pretty ,, Pretty in pink
Well She's Pretty ,, Pretty in pink

Copyright Jenny Dyer 16 March, 2015

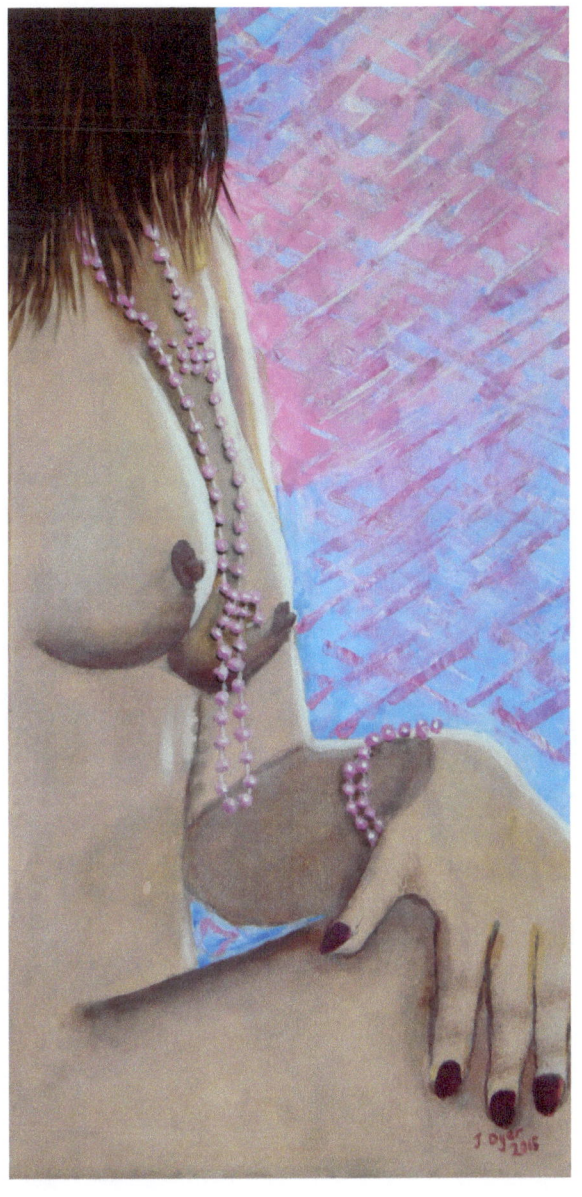

I was having fun with my art and I wanted to paint a few portraits. I'd never done a nude so I put it out to the world (yes on Facebook again my son) and a good friend offered to pose for me and I took her photo. I gave the painting to her and her husband and he loved it. Yes, before you say anything, I did ask her if it was alright to put in my book.

WHAT'S A FRIEND ANYWAY!!!
(For a change it's not a song but I wrote this then.)

Well I asked my Facebook friends for a hand (well photos of their hands actually) ... and this is what I ended up creating ... some made time to send me a photo of their hand or hands so I could do this painting. Not everyone, thank God, or I would have been painting the wall of the garage but enough to get my message across ... While I was painting I got to thinking about all the types of friends there are out there. Some won't have the time to read this but that's OK too.

There are so many friends you have haven't met yet
….There are friends who will write little inspirational notes to you, encourage you, support you, friends who convince you, you'll be right mate. There are friends who want to help you but don't know how unless you tell them and let them. There are friends that give and keep on giving, probably too much, but never asking or wanting anything in return. There are friends that give you the tools so you can help yourself … friends that give you direction so you know which way to turn next … There are friends that have travelled your path and know how difficult it is… and will be able to share their story so you know you aren't on your own. There are friends who reach out to help you that you know need help way more than you do … There are friends that will hold your hand through difficult times, lift you up when you fall. Friends that bring other friends into your life … share what they have. There are friends that cheer you up .. laugh with you… play with you. There are friends that share with you. There are friends that will teach you valuable life lessons, big and small. There are friends who reassure you when you need it and give you a pat on the back when you need it too. There are even friends that will lie to you because they know the truth will hurt too much!!

There are friends that are that busy getting their own lives together that they can't see others need a hand. There are even friends who don't know you need help unless you ask them and those that you know need help and won't ask but will take it if you offer and vice versa. Friends who know you have enough help. There are friends that don't help because they know you are better off doing it on your own.

Then there are those FRIENDS who hold your heart safely in their hands, keeping it warm until it glows with happiness. They just love you because really that's the most important thing a friend can give. You are one of the lucky ones if you have a friend or two like that. And hopefully in all this I hope I've been able to be that type of friend to the people in my life too.

As friends we aren't perfect (and I didn't paint those hands perfect either) but you know what, that doesn't matter .. No

one is perfect! And I think the painting has a message ….
Being not perfect is what makes life interesting, don't you
think? People's imperfect lives … and the imperfect
PERFECT friends they have.

OMG … that was philosophical, wasn't it (and it turned
into an essay … I think I could even add more … . So in all
those hours of painting you can see I was just thinking of
my friends … random thoughts cause that's how my poor
mind works … thinking of friends, some real close, some
not, some come into your life and some leave… but all play
a part, big or small, in my imperfect PERFECT life … love
them all. So thank you to all my friends … in all parts of
the world and know that you made a difference in my life.

This was one of the paintings I sadly sold. Hope that friend
is still happy with my painting and it reminds her of all the
friends she has.

Thank you for your encouragement.

Time for a break after all the philosophical talk. I'm
going walking with wildlife again.

God I Love That Smile

God I love that smile
She's looking at me
Long beautiful hair
Sweet as she can be

If you had the chance
You would see that too
Just from one glance
You would know its true

She's my beautiful girl
Sweetest woman in the world
She puts the light into my day
Better than any
Golden sun ray

Fresh as an ocean breeze
Such a gentle little soul
She'd do anything to please
She's got my starring role

Want to hold her
Want to hug her
Never want to let her go
I want to tell her
That I love her
But I think she already knows

She's my beautiful girl
Sweetest woman in the world
She puts the light into my day
Better than any
Golden sun ray

Better than any
Golden sun ray
Better than any
Golden sun ray

Copyright Jenny Dyer 12 October, 2014

Another song I changed so my music teacher could sing it. I really love this cheeky little number.

Got A Woman (Man)

*Scoop scopie do bah Barp barp and barp barp barp
Scoop scoop and barp barp barp Do bo and barp barp barp*

I got a woman **I got a woman**
She's alright **She's alright**
I got a woman **I got a woman**
Treats me real nice **Treats me real nice**

She's a home maker
Greets me at night **Greets me at night**
A sweet love maker **Sweet love maker**
That girl does it right **She does it right**

Say I got a woman **I got a woman**
She's waiting for me **Waiting for me**
I got a woman **I got a woman**
Makes me happy **she makes me happy**

I got a woman
Hard working **Hard working**
She understands **She understands me**
Won't see me hurting **Won't see me hurting**

I got a woman **Got a woman**
Neat as a pin **Gotta love him yeah**
I got a woman
Through thick or thin **Through thick and thin**

She makes me happy **She makes me happy**
Knows what to do **Knows what to do**
*Well I bet you wish you had
One like that too*

I got a woman **Got a woman**
Yes she's a keeper **She's a keeper**
I couldn't love her **I couldn't love her**
Lord any deeper **Lord any deeper**

Woah woah oh yeah **oh yeah**
This woman's a keeper **She's a keeper**
I couldn't love her **I couldn't love her**
Lord any deeper **Any deeper**

I got a woman **I got a woman**
She's alright ... **she's alright yeah**
I got a woman **I got a woman**
Treats me real nice real nice **oh yeah yeah yeah**

Cute homemaker
Greets me at night **Greets me at night**
She's a sweet lover maker **Sweet love maker**
Looks outta sight ... **looks outta site yeah**

I got a woman **I got a woman**
She's waiting for sin **Knows where to begin**
I got a woman **I got a woman**
Through Thick or thin **Thru thick and thin yeah yeah**

She makes me happy **Knows what to do**
You know bet you wish you had
One **like that too**
I got a woman **Got a woman**
She's alright **She's alright**
I got a woman **oh A woman yeah**
Treats me real nice **mmmm baby**

And she's a home maker
Greets me at night **Greets me at night**
A Sweet love maker **Sweet love maker**
That girl does it right **She does it right**

She's a sweet love maker **Sweet love maker**
That girl does it right **She does it right**
She's a sweet love maker **Sweet love maker**
That girl does it right **She does it right**
Oh that woman Ten out of ten
Perfection

Copyright Jenny Dyer 19 November, 2014

Just so you know I'm ready to get rid of that old piano. I really wanted to learn guitar but, of course my mother said "Girls don't play guitar". She had some funny ideas. You know I wasn't even allowed to wear jeans, wait for it, only loose girls wore jeans. So as soon as I left home I bought some jeans and also bought some for my little brother.

One of my favourite singers played guitar ... Suzy Q. She had spunk. I like that.

I remember singing one song by Nancy Sinatra called THESE BOOTS ARE MADE FOR WALKING ... "one day these boots are gunna walk all over you." I don't think I need the piano any more. I think it can go now. [OMG two hours past lunch time. I'm on a roll. Time to stop for a break.]

That Old Piano Heard My Tears

Just like a picture on the wall
That old piano has no use at all
Like granddaddy's dresser with the broken glass
Its just a memory of the past

No hope of being a big star
When my piano teacher only plays Bach
Mumma chose what I could do
Learning the classics is good for you

That old piano heard my tears
Followed me closely through the years
That old piano knows my heart
It's gunna be so hard to part

I was never the cool chick in town
Cause Bach wasn't the hip sound
I'd steal rock music sheets

Play those songs to my own beat.

Mumma knew what it meant to me
Heard me tinkering on the ivories
I'd write silly kid songs
When I was left home alone

That old piano heard my tears
Followed me closely through the years
That old piano knows my heart
Its gunna be so hard to part

That old piano has to go
It's only there just for show
The ivories have disappeared
A thing of the past don't show your tears

Just like a picture on the wall
That old piano has no use at all
Like granddaddy's dresser with the broken glass
Its just a memory of MY past

That old piano heard my tears
Followed me closely through the years
That old piano knows my heart
Its gunna be so hard to part
Just like a picture on the wall
That old piano has no use at all

Copyright Jenny Dyer 4 September, 2014

Looks like I'm going to have another clean out. My daughter cleaned out the art room last time she came home to visit. I've sold my art material. I don't need them any more. My music and art were there when I needed it. Now it's time to move on to more important things … Grandkids, they are so special and my bucket list.

Maybe the garage next time where my old piano is. What a waste! I may give my piano away on Facebook.

Sweet Soul King Of The Blues

Last night I heard those guitars cry
The King of the blues he up and died
No one could make a guitar sing
Like the great BB King

I could feel the chill in the air
I was listening to the thrill
Oh yeah he has gone
Played his last song and he was gone

**Oh BB it don't get much bluer than this
And if I had one more wish
I'd play a few bars with you
Sweet soul king of the blues**

His spirit rose as my fire was burning
His spark has gone, won't be returning
He belonged to that master class
So I filled up my glass

I had to make one last toast
Do you think we'll be hearing BB's ghost
In the words of tribute songs
Yeah BB's gone.

CHORUS

Yeah his time was up
Happens to the best of us
So dear Lord have mercy
We'll pray that he's worthy

Pray he don't need no key to that highway
Cause he'll be flying today
He'll have those harps jamming
When he makes his landing

CHORUS

Copyright Jenny Dyer May 15, 2015

RANDOM THOUGHT You know when I don't want songs to interrupt my thoughts I listen to instrumentals because that is what is playing in the background right now. So easy to concentrate.. This book I'm writing is so soul cleansing. You were right, True Blue, when you said, "You've got a soul that needs cleansing".

Now the reason for the BLEEDING ROSES …. This painting was called "Innocence" (a white rose) see page 7 shown earlier in the book. I later defaced another painting as I wrote the song to go with it.

Left Bleeding And Hurt (Who Can A Kid Turn To?)

Do you know how scary it is
To be left bleeding and hurt
To know what was done was so wrong
A band-aid won't cover that hurt

Who can a kid turn to
Scared to be in trouble
Wondering if they're gunna die
No longer feeling lovable

The things he made her do
Have shadowed her husband's love
She had to use mind control
When he gave her a hug

35 years she did that
Till one day she exploded
Just couldn't keep it under her hat
Her armour had corroded

Those corrugations of life
Are rarely talked about
But could you imagine being a wife
Living under that shroud

Do you know how scary it is
To be left bleeding and hurt
To know what was done was so wrong
A band-aid won't cover that hurt

Who can a kid turn to
Scared to be in trouble
Wandering if they're gunna die
No longer feeling lovable

Copyright Jenny Dyer June19, 2015

Then I wrote the following song. My music teacher/my best friend, was very selective about what he recorded. He would only record the songs that had a good positive message.

I Feel Good

I feel strong I feel happy
Is it a shame that the only words that rhymes..
.. with happy … is crappy

I feel good I feel alive
You know I write my songs to stay alive

I feel strong I feel happy
I feel good I feel alive - yeah

I feel strong Mmmmm
I'm feelin happy
Don't I feel good ………..
Isn't it great to feel alive

I feel like dancing
I feel like romancing
But the one I love is miles away
I feel like hugging
I feel like kissing
But I pick up my guitar and play

But I still feel strong
And I still feel happy
And I still feel good
Isn't it great to feel alive

My man he won't be home for two weeks
I'm a little lonely need some cheek to cheek
He's in the outback camping in the scrub
Can't wait to get me some of his love
Can't wait to get me some of his love

Oh I feel strong
Mmmm Yeh I'm feelin happy
Don't I feel good ………..
Isn't it great to feel alive
Isn't it great to feel alive
Isn't it great to feel alive

Copyright Jenny Dyer June 24, 2015

The straw that broke the camel's back

I heard it on the news! Rolf Harris was charged with sexual abuse. I got so angry that I threw myself into a painting. I really was passing on the anger I had for the person who hurt me. But I couldn't put his picture in my painting. I would have had to look into those eyes.

I later heard Harris was charged for abusing 25 children. I immediately thought what if HE (my abuser) went on to abuse more girls after me. I DIDN'T SPEAK OUT. I was so angry, shocked and devastated. It would be all my fault for not speaking up earlier so I diverted my anger to myself this time ... is there always more than one victim? Are all sexual predators repeat offenders?

Then I defaced the painting to show all his victims! That is 25 young people's lives he destroyed. I wonder if it affected them like me. I guess I'll never know.

The song I wrote about this isn't worth sharing ... too much anger ... I had shown enough anger with the painting and I really don't want to remember that in my old age. (I just went back and read the song. I changed my mind so here it is. You really have to listen to this one so load it up to listen while you read.)

BURN BROTHER BURN

Sometimes you gotta hide your feelings
People don't need to know
Can't cope with what life is dealing
Hope it doesn't show

Feel so weak and I'm struggling
Let things get under my skin
Time to give myself a slapping
And take those things on my chin

There's a lot of anger in that picture
Lot of anger waiting to show
I kept it under control
For how long I don't know
So burn brother burn
All up in smoke
Burn brother burn
I'll teach you
My feelings are no joke

Take that picture into the garden
Chop it with an axe
Throw those pieces in the fire pit
As I sip a wine and relax

How many years has it been
Maybe its time for you to learn
How much anger I've kept in
I'll make you watch it burn

There's a lot of anger in that picture
Lot of anger waiting to show
I kept it under control
For how long I don't know
So burn brother burn
All up in smoke
Burn brother burn
I'll teach you
My feelings are no joke

Copyright Jenny Dyer 22 October, 2014

Tribute to my music teacher

When I wrote songs, I'd show them to my husband but he wasn't interested in reading my silly songs. Not being a musician, he didn't understand they were my deepest thoughts and feelings, He didn't understand how hurt I was.

One person listened to every word I wrote… my music teacher. He knew where it was all coming from.

He listened to me singing the songs (very poorly but he didn't judge). Then he would eagerly grab his guitar and sometimes change my chords, well almost always changed the chords to make the songs better because music was his specialty not mine. I loved the way he listened, asked questions, sometimes gave advice and took my words of pain, anger and love and make them sound so good with him and/or Claire singing. I was so grateful to them both.

He knew more about songwriting and hurt than any of the psychologists that I later worked with knew. They weren't even interested in reading my songs either. They didn't even know my songs were the only way I could communicate and verbalise the hurt I had inside. I just couldn't face talking about it.

I wrote so many songs for him too because I was so grateful to have such a good friend. Thank you so much for being my guardian angel. It was also a highlight listening to his music when he would perform at different events. I can remember finding a song especially for him while I was trolling music on YouTube "I'm sexy and I know it". He had such a good sense of humour and often changed the word "I" to an audience member's name. Always good for a laugh and a great entertainer as well.

This painting hung in his studio for years.

I loved live music

I never had access to live music when I was young. At college I couldn't afford to go to see it. Then I went out west to teach in a little town in outback Queensland where there was no live music. When I came back to civilization I had small children. Then work also took my time.

I'd take the photos of the performers and then paint them with feeling because I just loved the memory.

The vibration coming from that big gold guitar (on next page) was something else. I could feel them through the floor. I wish I could have gone to more music festivals but the memory of the music festivals and the performances will stay with me forever. I dragged my poor husband along. Not his thing but he put up with it.

Thank You Lord For Giving Me This

Sitting in the morning sun
Watching the birds flying around
Last night was a bit of fun
Away from this sleepy old town

We headed down south
In the back of a coaster bus
Davie and his girl were driving
With all fourteen of us

Blues and bourbon the choice for the trip
Cracked the top of a few
I was only taking a sip
But a sip just wouldn't do

This wind's a bit of a chill
Gotta be telling you this
Before I get over the hill I wanta
Thank you Lord for giving me this

Pulled up at the Waterhole
The crowd was building strong
I wanna hear Spiegel sing
His "who do you love" song

Chose a meal from the diner
Ordered a wine or three
Listened to some old timer
And his harp playing wannabe

This wind's a bit of a chill
Gotta be telling you this
Before I get over the hill I wanta
Thank you Lord for giving me this
Thank you Lord for giving me this

The star act came on stage
His fingers lightning fast
This gig's just come of age
Lift the spirit of the poor downcast

24 miles of barbed wire
Just couldn't tie me down
Who do you love just has to be
The craziest song round

This wind's a bit of a chill
Gotta be telling you this
Before I get over the hill I wanta
Thank you Lord for giving me this
Thank you Lord for giving me this

This wind's a bit of a chill
Gotta be telling you this
Before I get over the hill I wanta
Thank you Lord for giving me this
Thank you Lord for giving me this

Copyright Jenny Dyer   July 29, 2015

Grandchildren on the Way

My song for ALL of them.

I'd Like To Believe

I'd like to believe you will live
In a world full of peace
I'd like to believe you will live
With love that will never cease

I'd like to believe you will live
Where people can be free
I'd like to believe you will live
And always be happy

Not scared of the dark
Not afraid to make your mark
Free of hunger and pain
Where love and compassion reign
Oh yeah I'd like to believe
I'd like to believe (to believe)

I'd like to believe you will live
On adventure and fun
I'd like to believe you will live
Through all seasons of the sun

I'd like to believe you will live
And be taught the ropes
I'd like to believe you will live
Never losing hope

Not scared of the dark
Not afraid to make your mark
Free of hunger and pain
Where love and compassion reign
Oh yeah I'd like to believe
I'd like to believe (to believe)

BRIDGE
I'd like to believe
You'll do the best you possibly can
I'd like to believe
You'll love and understand
So before I lay me down to rest
I'd like to see you at your best
I'd like to see you love and learn
And know which way you're gunna turn

Not scared of the dark
Not afraid to make your mark
Free of hunger and pain
Where love and compassion reign
Oh yeah I'd like to believe
I'd like to believe (to believe)
I'd like to believe
I'd like to believe
Oh I'd like to believe
I'd like to believe I'd like to believe

Copyright Jenny Dyer August 31, 2015

Sweet Little Boy

Just the other day
I saw the most precious thing
The love in my heart oh
Makes me want to sing
A beautiful child
Born to my son
A beautiful child
HE'S GOT MY HEART WON

He's a real miracle
Yes he brings such joy
Our little Baby Will
Our sweet little boy

It seems like yesterday
When I welcomed my own son
Now he's here holding
His own little one.

A tiny little babe
Doesn't want for much
He eats and he sleeps
And receives such love.

He's a real miracle
Yes he brings such joy
Our little Baby Will
Our sweet little boy

He's a real miracle
I'll tell you again
The world is at his feet
He's our little man

He's a real miracle
Yes he brings such joy
Our little Baby Will
Our sweet little boy
Our little Baby Will
Our sweet little boy

Copyright Jenny Dyer February 22, 2016

Amazing Little Grace

Amazing little Grace
A name so sweet
A lovely babe like you
A little girl
Ever so petite
Oh how they'll love you

Perfect little hands
And perfect toes
What a joy you will bring
Rose petals lips
A button nose
Just perfect everything

Sweet little child
Born today .. Well I'm
Glad to see you're alright
Your Mum and Dad
I'm pleased to say
Had an angel in the night

I'm sitting here
Watching from afar
I wait for pictures of you
I can't wait
My shining star
Can't wait to cuddle you.

Amazing little Grace
A name so sweet
A lovely babe like you
A little girl
Ever so petite
Oh how they'll love you

Oh how they'll love you
Oh how they'll love you

Copyright Jenny Dyer March 1, 2016

I wrote this after my mother passed.

She Loved Me Like No Other

She prayed for me when I was bad
Cried for me when I was sad
Walked with me when times were tough
Held my hand when the road got rough

It's with sadness that we watch her go
We'll miss her more than you'll know
Oh to feel one last kiss
Or the embrace that we will miss

CHORUS
She loved me like no other
She's the angel I call mother
She loved me like no other
She looked after me
So selflessly

Jesus, she's on her way to you
All pretty dressed in blue
Can you hold her tightly for me
And just kiss her tenderly

Greet her with her friends
This is her beginning not her end
Take her in to your home
So she won't be alone

CHORUS

I have just one prayer
For the angel who cared
In you Lord she had faith
So please keep her safe

CHORUS

Copyright Jenny Dyer November 15, 2016

Tribute to my husband

You also had to go through a lot on your own. You're a strong man. I am so grateful to have to you by my side. I love you. Don't you ever forget, or else!!! Remember my song for your 60th birthday.

Come Closer

You're the Mona Lisa to my art
You're the veins to my heart
You're the Lennon to my songs
With you I can't go wrong

You're the bounce to my step
You're my future not seen yet
You're the sparkle to my stars
I'm happy wherever you are.

**Come closer, I want to breathe you in
Come closer, skin on skin
Come closer, take your time
Hold your body next to mine (next to mine next to mine)**

You're the colour to my sky (come closer)
You're the twinkle in my eye
You're the rose among my thorns (come closer)
You're my home in a storm

You're the comfort to my pain (come closer)
And I'm sure you feel the same
You're the light in my sun (come closer)
Without you life's no fun

**Come closer, I want to breathe you in
Come closer, skin on skin
Come closer, take your time
Hold your body next to mine.**

You're the food to my soul (come closer)
Without you life would be cold
You're my shelter when afraid (come closer)
You're my love that never fades

Always there when things are tough (come closer)
And I'm hanging for your love
To me you are everything (come closer)
That's why I wear your ring

Come closer, I want to breathe you in
Come closer, skin on skin
Come closer, take your time
Hold your body next to mine.
Hold your body next to mine.
Hold your body next to mine.

Copyright Jenny Dyer March 2014

One Woman One Man

One woman one man
They made a promise
One woman one man
They would be honest
One woman one man
Living together
One woman one man
Promised forever

CHORUS
That has to be magic
That has to be trust
That has to be love til
Ashes and dust
That has to be love til
Ashes and dust

One woman one man
That's all it takes
One woman one man
A marriage it makes

One woman one man
That's all it would be
One woman one man
Till eternity

CHORUS

One woman one man
That was their dream
One woman one man
She remained his queen

CHORUS

Copyright Jenny Dyer   July 18 2016

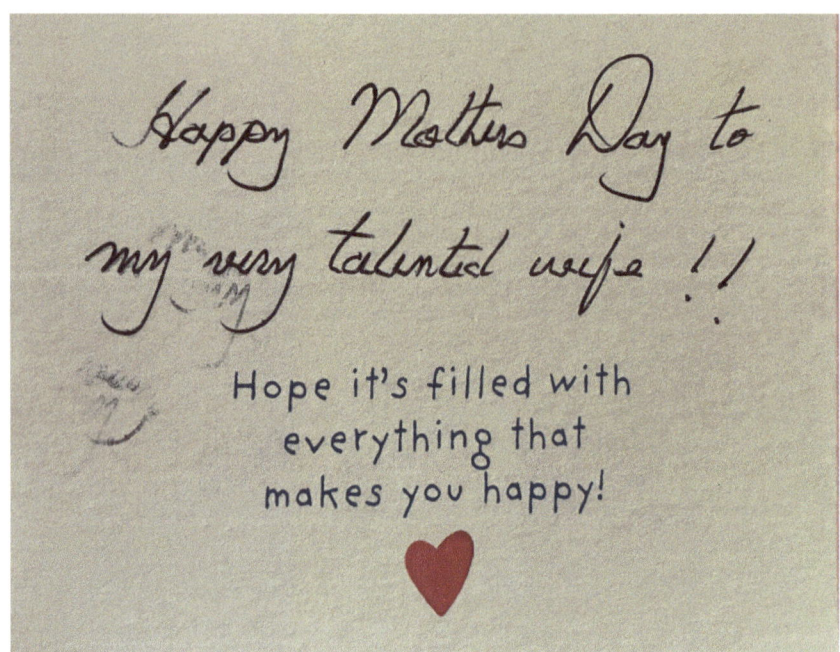

The last thing on my old Bucket List was to see my granddaughter my Amazing Little Grace. I forgot to write another bucket list!.

My old art/music room has just been cleaned out. I have stopped painting and singing and now I've just revisited my life with music and art. I lived through all of it and now am back doing what I loved doing in my imagination as a kid .... photographing my beautiful homeland and the animals and birds, then writing children's stories about it and spending time with my grandchildren.

Our grandchildren will inherit this land and I'm hoping they see how amazing it is and endeavour to keep it that way for generations to come.

If you are reading this book, it's because my husband and children made the decision and thought my story was worth telling the world even though it wasn't always bright and rosy. (I wanted to use a pen name to hide my identity but my songs are already out there for the world to see). Sometimes you just have to own it!

I love both my children and I love my beautiful grandchildren but most of all, I love my husband who put up with me for all these years. What is it? Let me do the Maths - 46 years! That's longer than you get for murder.

I'm on a roll. I'm nearly finished but I really do need to go pee. (old age)

One red rose for the man who stood by me through all the hard times as well as the good ... I love you.

My New Bucket List

1. Write a story about my youngest beautiful grandchild called "Henry travels the world. " (He missed having a song written about him because he wasn't thought of when I was writing my songs).
2. Finish my Walking with Wildlife series to teach children about the miracles of nature and that nature can be cruel.
3. Finish this memoir for my children and grandchildren to read when they're ready and maybe have it made into a musical. YEP, I'm still a dreamer.
4. Write a story for little children to read to show them what to do if someone tries to hurt them. Yes it needs to be spoken about in your home. I would like a free printable E-book and a printed one as well. (not free) I need someone to pay for those books. I can't afford it.
5. Write a story called "The Mouse in My House" which is about being kind to living creatures and to shut the damn doors in my house so they can't get in. I found the lyrics in my archives and thought it would make a good kids' story.
6. Make sure my family know how very much I love them.
7. Have a weekend away with nature with my family for my 70th. I can't travel too far with my sore back otherwise I'd be going to Africa to photograph the amazing animals.
8. Enjoy the company of friends each week while I still can.
9. Cuddle my grandchildren's children. Sorry kids, I'm around for a while or maybe you'll have to finish that one for me.
10. Maybe get my kids to carry on the tradition and write their bucket list and keep on writing them. We're only here for a speck of time.

Now to tick them off one by one. Not my family ... the list!

THE END OR A NEW BEGINNING.

After thoughts

Life is fragile. Life can be cruel. I was going to title this book BROKEN BUT STRONG, but I changed my mind. (A woman's prerogative.) Did I use the right title? Is there power in those hands? If I push myself too hard will I crack? It's a real tight rope I'm walking but I'm glad I've written this memoir. Here's to new beginnings.

I'm looking after myself and that's why I go WALKING WITH WILDLIFE daily. I need to do more. I'm not a singer, I'm not a good painter, I may not write hit songs but I do have real feelings. Be kind! I'm still following my dreams. Don't choke my creativity or things will be left unfinished.   It's the creative people in the world that challenge society to think.   Will I ever find out what I'm meant to do or have I already done it? **Your choice!**

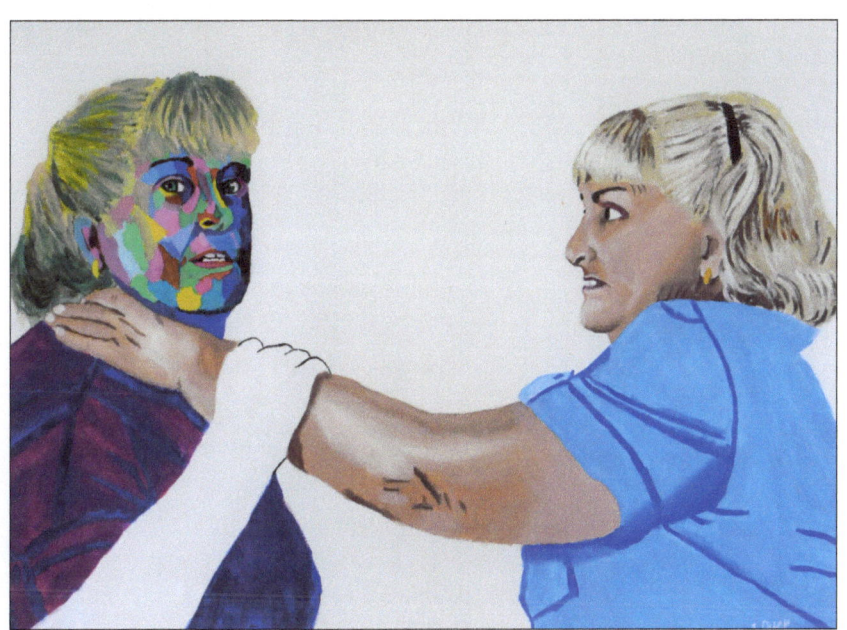

PS I found one last important song after taking my trip through my old song lyrics. I think this may be one of the most important songs. Forgiveness is the key, it will set you free.

That Girl In The Mirror (Forgiveness is the Key)

That girl in the mirror doesn't know what to do
She doesn't know how to forgive you
It's too late the words have been spoken
It's too late the trust has been broken

That girl in the mirror's looking back at me
Telling me not to be so angry
Telling me that forgiveness is the key
To moving on and setting her free

Forgiveness is the key
It will set you free
Forgive yeah forgive and let live
The only thing you can give
Just forgive, yeah forgive and let live
Forgive yeah forgive forgive

That girl in the mirror with such intense eyes
Keeps on asking, why why why
Why did you have to scar her heart
Why did you play such a part

That girl in the mirror she looks so sad
She keeps thinking about all that she had
She misses everything that she has lost
The truth is out but at what cost

Forgiveness is the key
It will set you free
Forgive yeah forgive and let live
The only thing you can give
Just forgive, yeah forgive and let live
Forgive yeah forgive forgive

That girl in the mirror doesn't know what to do
She doesn't know whether to believe you
You said sorry didn't mean to cause pain
If you could you'd take it back again.

That girl in the mirror doesn't like the memory
That you entrenched in her history
They say forgiveness is the precious key
To moving on and setting her free.

Copyright Jenny Dyer September 2012
Saved as: song-That Girl in the Mirror

I'm done, I'm finished
I don't need to write songs any more
But I will use those skills
to write children's books galore.

Good communication is the key.

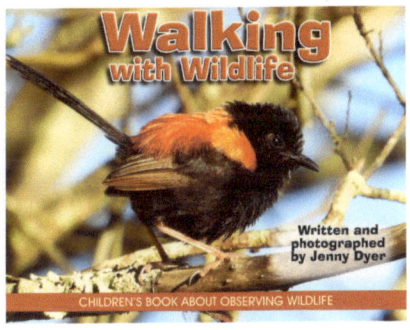
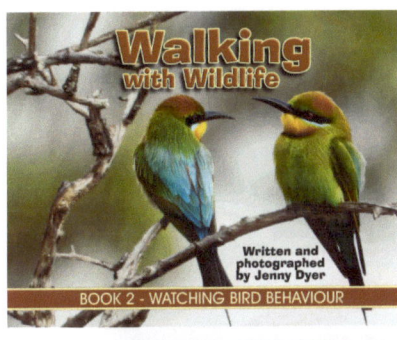

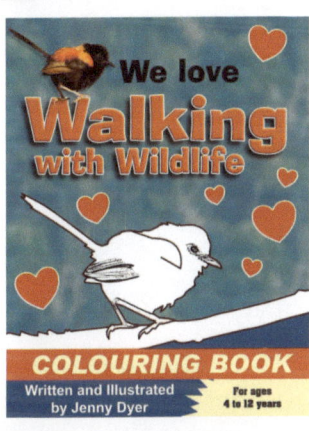
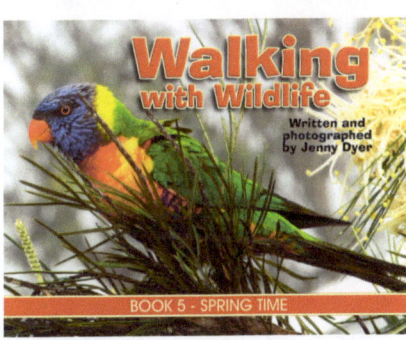
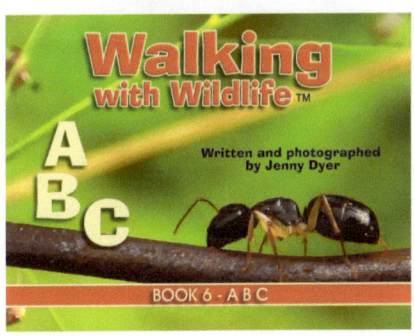
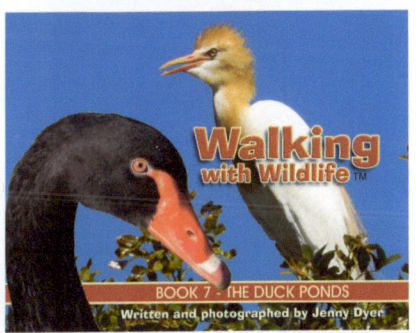

The start of my series of books

www.walkingwithwildlife.com.au

www.ingramcontent.com/pod-product-compliance
Lightning Source LLC
Chambersburg PA
CBHW042225090526
44583CB00001BA/1